1980

Coins,
Collectors,
and
Counterfeiters

Coins, Collectors, and Counterfeiters

by
Edwin P. Hoyt

THOMAS NELSON INC., PUBLISHERS
Nashville   New York

First edition

Library of Congress Cataloging in Publication Data
Hoyt, Edwin Palmer.
  Coins, collectors, and counterfeiters.
  Bibliography: p.
  Includes index.
  1. Numismatics—History. 2. Counterfeits and counterfeiting—
History. I. Title.
CJ59.H69   737.4'09   76-58015
ISBN 0-8407-6537-1

Contents

Coins,
Collectors,
and
Counterfeiters

1
The Story of Coinage

Coin collecting is different from almost any other hobby, because coins have value as metal, too. There have always been people who hoarded valuable coins chiefly for their monetary worth.

This fact has been both the salvation and the bane of the true coin collector. The value of various kinds of money has kept that money from being destroyed, but the inherent value of coined money also has brought about speculation, hoarding, theft, dishonesty, and violence, to say nothing of so many varieties of counterfeiting that many books have been devoted to that subject alone.

In the Fertile Crescent, the region in the Middle East where civilization began, the major standard of value was at first the cow or ox, and sometimes the sheep or goat, and thus many of the words having to do with money come from such stems. The word *pecunia* is Latin for "money," and it comes from *pecus,* which means a single head of cattle. So we have *pecuniary,* which means monetary. Our word "capital" comes from the Latin *caput,* or "head."

Old and strange varieties of money will be described in this book, for they have their collectors, just as coins do. But coins were something else again, something special, and it was thousands of years after the beginnings of civilization before men refined their thinking to the point where they adopted the sets of values necessary for the beginning of coinage.

Any coin is the result of much thought. It is a piece of metal of a specific weight and fineness, which bears the mark of the government or the authority that issued it. That mark guarantees the genuine nature and value of the coin, the weight and the fineness of the metal.

Coins came into use in about the year 700 B.C. in Lydia, now a part of Turkey but then one of the city-states that made up Greater Greece. These first coins were made of an alloy of gold and silver, which was natural because gold and silver are often found together, and primitive smelting processes were unlikely to separate the metals. This mixture was called electrum. Later, it was learned that electrum consisted of gold and silver and that the proportions were not always the same. When it became apparent that gold was more valuable than silver (because it was scarcer), the electrum coins soon went out of fashion. But in the beginning, this was the metal of coinage. The unit coined was a stater. It was equivalent in weight to two drachmas of silver, or about eight grams. It was oval in shape, with one side marked by irregular lines (caused by the anvil on which it was placed) and the other side deeply indented by a royal stamp, which represented a lion.

About 150 years after the invention of the stater, King Croesus of Lydia began making coins of pure gold and others of pure silver. He revolutionized coinage. Other city-states had learned how to make coins from the Lydians, but they had not learned to separate and purify the metals. The Lydian coins then became the most valuable in all the Greek states, and Lydia thus became an important political power. Soon the secret of silver and gold coinage was out, however, and all the Greek states began making standard coins. Two or three hundred years later, the idea of coinage had spread far east and west.

The Chinese came upon the idea of coinage independently, as they came upon so many other ideas independently of the West, but it is known that the expeditions of conquest carried out by Darius of Persia and Alexander the Great of Macedon brought coins into use in much of what is now the Middle East and northern Africa. Several hundred years before the birth of Christ, coins were in common use throughout the Egyptian world and the civilizations that abutted Egypt, and particularly in the dominant Greek world. But of course nobody was collecting them then. The most that could be said was that some people hoarded coins against a rainy day. It was good that they did. Their greed provided much excitement for future nations, for every once in a while, even into the middle of the twentieth century, someone would be digging and would find a hoard of ancient coins, no longer valuable as pieces of money, but invaluable, some of them, as collector's items.

It seems hard to believe, but many coins that were in use in the ancient world of Greece are still available, even to modest private collectors. From time to time somewhere in the Greek islands new coins are unearthed to add to the collection—although not as quickly as growing prosperity in the world has added to the number of collectors. In that ancient world, if anyone had been interested in collecting the coins of the world, it would have been hard for him to decide how and what to collect. Among the Greek city-states alone there were more than 120,000 different varieties of coins.

The Greeks improved very quickly on the Lydian method of making coins. Instead of striking a metal disk with an engraved tool, they placed the disk between two engraved dies and then put it on the anvil and hit it with a hammer to make the dies penetrate the soft, valuable metal.

The basic unit of value in Greece was the talent of silver, which was valued about $1,125. A talent contained sixty minas. (Each mina was about a pound of silver.) A mina consisted of a hundred drachmas, and so a drachma was worth about 20 cents. This seemed to be the most sensible, workable unit for coinage, and it was handed down, generally speaking, in the French franc, Italian lira, Swedish krone, and British shilling. It was much more valuable, however.

Even a few years ago, before the silver content was modified, few people would think of forging an American quarter or a British shilling. But in Ancient Greece, the 20-

cent drachma was a valuable coin. A man who earned five hundred drachmas a year was a rich man. A drachma would buy a sheep, five drachmas would buy a cow. There was so much cheating on the mixture of gold and silver in the electrum coins going on that with the emergence of Athens as the cultural leader of Greece, the silver coin became the standard. The Spartans, for a time, used iron currency. It was very bulky for its value, but that was the idea—to make money so hard to use that the people would not think in terms of goods and luxuries.

During the days of Philip of Macedon, father of Alexander the Great, the Macedonian tetradrachm, which was much like our dollar, found its way as far afield as Britain, by traveling through the Danube River Valley into northern Europe, and as far as Iceland. Then, when Alexander became king and extended his empire, he took Greek coinage to the ends of the known earth, and in great quantities. In 1905 a lucky group of diggers in the Middle East unearthed eight thousand of Alexander's tetradrachmas, with the head of Heracles on one side and the seated figure of the god Zeus with eagle and thunderbolt on the other. This treasure had been buried in 318 B.C., at a time when it represented the fortune of a kingdom.

Between the days of the Greeks and the days of the Romans, conditions changed, and values changed markedly. For example, the measure, the talent, jumped in value to $6,000 in our money, and the purchasing power of Roman money changed accordingly. Roman power extended for a much longer period than Greek power. Rome became much wealthier, and its influence spread farther. Greek coins can be collected by individuals, but any sizable collection soon runs into something costly. This was not true of Roman coins, even during the middle of the twentieth century, for so many have been found that for a few dollars anyone could begin such a collection. During the 1960's one could buy a Julius Caesar denarius, worth about a dollar in its time, for ten dollars. This coin showed an elephant trampling on a dragon on one side, with a ax, sprinkler, and ladle on the other. It is believed to have been struck in 54 B.C. in order to finance the Gallic Wars. In the 1970's it was two thousand years old, and the values had risen sharply. Indeed, between 1970 and 1975, the increase in number of coin collectors sent values up about 400 percent over the past.

The first Roman coin was made in the fourth century before the birth of Christ, about two hundred years after the Greeks began using coins. The Romans were aware of the Greek coins, because Greek civilization had spread to the Roman boot. Still, until 400 B.C. the Romans used lumps of bronze as a medium of exchange. Then came the coin known as the as, in Latin, *aes grave*. It weighed one Roman pound in the beginning. (Supposedly it was the ancestor of the British pound, which once truly weighed a pound.) The front—or *obverse* side—of the as showed a portrait of the god Janus, a two-faced god worshiped by the Romans as the god of gods. The other side—or *reverse*—was stamped with a picture of a ship and the figure 1, which meant that this coin was worth one of the old pieces of bronze. The as was the basic Roman unit of currency for two hundred years. In the third century before the birth of Christ, Rome's military victories became so extensive that the coinage was changed from bronze to silver. The defeat of Pyrrhus and Hasdrubal, the conquest of Greater Greece, the spoils of Tarentum, the plunder of Sardinia, all brought thousands of talents of silver into Rome, so much silver that the Romans decided to change their system of coinage, and did so in 269 B.C. This led to the coinage of the *denarius* and the *sesterce,* which was a quarter of a denarius.

The establishment of the Roman coining system of 269 B.C. had much to do with the growing power of Rome and the emergence of Rome as *the* conqueror of the world. Rome's money became an international standard. One of the problems of coinage in Rome's conquests was to make enough coins to meet the demands from Gaul to Jerusalem. Mints were established in various parts of the Roman world. In the mints coins were made by use of the hammer, shears, and file. A workman could make only about twenty coins a day, so there had to be many mints or places of coinage of money. The Roman Senate had some trouble keeping these mints under control. But they managed, and the Romans established the first real financial system. The chief financial officers were censors, appointed to buy bullion or seize it from captive states. (After the capture of Carthage at the end of the First Punic War, Lutatius Catullus forced Carthage to pay 2,200 talents of silver to Rome each year for twenty years.) Also under the Senate came the quaestors, who paid government debts. The mints themselves were under control of three triumvirs, who supervised the slaves who made the coins.

Rome's Senate manipulated the money of Rome, and devalued it from time to time by cutting down the amount of silver in the coins. At one time, during the wars against Carthage, the amount of silver was reduced by 80 percent. Consequently the word "denarius" has no standard meaning to coin collectors of the twentieth century, regarding the amount of silver in a coin (no more so than "dollar" or "quarter" has anymore).

The system of *mintmarks* was begun to show where any given group of coins had been made. Partly this was for the protection of the coiners, but equally it was for the protection of the public, to be sure that the coiners did not debase the money, stealing the silver and putting base metals into the coins instead. This was a common practice among coiners, if they felt they could get away with it.

The conquests by the Roman Republic brought so many riches into Rome that the Romans paid no taxes for support of their government or their armies. The armies often supported themselves in the field. During the days of the Republic, the generals obtained the right to make coins of their own, because it was so difficult to transport supplies and so dangerous to send money to the places where the legions were stationed. Sulla, Pompey, Caesar, and other generals coined their own money as far back as the first century B.C., and these coins had an effect that no one anticipated.

Coinage was the symbol of power. The followers of these Roman generals began to regard the generals as more powerful than the Senate itself.

Since there were so many Roman coiners, each of them interested in commemorating his own great deeds and those of his relatives and friends, Roman coins tell the history of the Roman Republic. But the number of varieties was soon diminished. About 100 B.C. the barbarians threatened Rome from the north, and the generals Marius and Sulla fought them to a standstill, then fought each other. From this carnage arose the figure of Julius Caesar.

Caesar conquered the barbarians of Gaul, then came back to Rome with his army and seized power over the Republic. One of his first acts was to seize the power of coinage. Here, he knew, lay a primary power of the state on its citizens.

Caesar issued many coins in honor of his various victories. Eventually, in 44 B.C., he ordered a coin issued that bore his own likeness. This self-adulation was very much against public policy in Rome. Never before had a coin borne the likeness of a living person. By this act Caesar was telling the world that he was not simply a living person but a god. The coin helped bring about his downfall. One month after this coin was struck, Caesar was assassinated by his friend Brutus and Caesar's jealous rivals.

There are very few gold coins in the Roman coinage, but one of them was struck shortly after the assassination of Caesar. It indicated the state of affairs in Rome at that moment. It bore a picture of Brutus on the obverse side and a cap of liberty and two daggers on the reverse. Later this coin was also issued in silver.

Now all the leaders of Rome who came to power issued coins with their likenesses on them, and coins became a part of the power struggle. Mark Antony opposed Octavian for power after the two of them had joined with Lepidus in a triumvirate. In 32 B.C. Antony created a master propaganda stroke by issuing eighteen different silver denarii, each honoring one of his eighteen legions. By so doing he made his legions so famous throughout the area controlled by Rome that he secured the support of many lesser kings, who were impressed by this display of wealth and power. He was finally defeated by Octavian at Actium. Octavian assumed the title of Caesar Augustus, became the first Roman emperor, and issued coins to cement his power.

The days of Octavian-Augustus mark the great change in Rome, and the coins show it.

The coinage of Rome is divided into two parts—that of the Republic, which includes the last coins of Antony, and the coinage of the Empire, which begins when Octavian assumed the role of emperor. One of his first acts as Augustus was to establish eighteen government mints at various points in the empire. He alone controlled those mints.

Augustus was followed by Tiberius, who was followed by Caligula, by Claudius, and then by Nero, after Claudius was poisoned by his wife Agrippina. It is all shown in Rome's coins. Nero is often given credit—or blame—for perfecting the debasement of coinage. He was not the first or the last to add lead to the denarii and pocket the silver left out of the coins. In the world of the twentieth century, all governments have debased coinage to the point that the original concept of value is meaningless.

The silver coins of Augustus were 100 percent pure. Those of Nero were 90 percent pure. This lasted until about 50 A.D. From that point on, affairs worsened rapidly. Under Trajan the silver content dropped to 85

18

percent. Then in 211, Caracalla signaled the end of good money by introducing a coin called the antoninianus, which had a silver content of only 50 percent. Forty years later the silver content had dropped to 5 percent. In 284 there was only 2 percent silver in the coin, in the form of a silver wash, which very quickly wore off, leaving a base-metal coin that was trusted by no one.

The gold coins of the Empire were to fall into almost as sad a state. The bronze as, which had been a pound in weight in the original days of the Republic, had fallen to a quarter of an ounce by Nero's time, although attempts were made to say that it was the same coin, in terms of purchasing power. What was happening? Rome had reached the end of her days of conquest.

She had taken and wasted all the loot of her old enemies and friends and colonies. She had destroyed the productivity of the silver mines in Spain and Gaul. Precious metals could no longer be gained by conquest, and as the coinage was debased, the well-to-do and even the peasants buried the old, good money in the ground to save against days of disaster. So the phrase "bad money drives out good" became a reality, and soon few good coins could be found in circulation in the Roman empire. By the time of the Emperor Gallienus, around 260, silver coins had nearly disappeared, and bronze coins were in use. These later Roman bronze coins were very plentiful and in the 1970's were still relatively inexpensive, although they were more than fifteen hundred years old by then.

The common people soon caught on to the tricks of their rulers and sometimes outfoxed them. In 284 when Diocletian became emperor, matters had grown so serious that the *follis,* a large bronze coin washed with silver, was introduced. It fooled no one. People took the follis, shook a number of them together in a bag to rub off the silver, then carried them into the towns and exchanged them for new coins, and did the same thing over again.

Coins continued to be a document to history. The Roman empire split in 306 when Constantine the Great transferred his seat of power to Constantinople. There he issued the first coin to bear a Christian symbol—the Greek letters Chi and Rho, the initial letters of "Christ."

2
The Coins of Europe

1. England

One reason why the Greeks and Romans had so much trouble in keeping coins within their city-states, republics, and kingdoms was that the barbarians who did not manufacture any coins of their own soon learned to value these pieces of metal, and they took them off into northern Europe as media of exchange. The first coin to be so used seems to have been the gold stater minted in 350 B.C. and afterward by Philip of Macedon. The Greek colony at Marseilles introduced this coin into Gaul. Soon the Gauls were copying the coin, although they paid very little attention to the basic requirement of coinage for maintenance of value—the specific weight of specific metal. Also, most of the early barbarian copies of the coins of Greece and Rome were so crude that they could hardly be recognized as coins at all. Other coins were copies, among them the silver tetradrachm of Thasos, which was issued around 150 B.C. Some of these copies came down to modern times. They are valuable as curiosities.

When Rome took ascendance over Gaul and the Germanic regions, the coins of the Roman Republic, of the generals, and of the emperors soon found their way north —again helping create the coin shortage in Rome itself. The barbarians hoarded Roman coins for wealth and copied them for use in their own trade. When the Byzantine Empire was established at Constantinople, and the Roman coinage was so badly debased, the barbarians took to using the coins of the Eastern Emperors, and thus the *bezant,* the coin of the Byzantines, became the standard gold coin of the Western World during all the Dark Ages.

The first truly northern European coin was devised in the days of Charlemagne. In about 800 A.D., when the Holy Roman Empire was formed for the protection of Christian Europe, Charlemagne approached the monetary problem with the same eye that the Romans and other coiners had used. He established a pound of silver as the basis of value of his coinage, and this pound of silver was divided into 240 *deniers.* A silver coin by that name was coined. So was another silver coin, called a *solidus,* which had the value of 12 deniers. There were 20 solidi in a pound of silver. This became the standard of European coinage and eventually the basis for British coinage until the 1970's, when Britain went to the metric monetary system.

The British developed their own coinage, in scanty supply, very early. One British numismatist, Sir John Evans, says the British established a mint at Kent as early as 150 B.C., producing coins that were a crude imitation of the stater of Philip of Macedon. Some of these coins were made of silver, some of gold, some of a mixture of these metals, and some of copper. An important discovery of such coins was made in 1885 at Freckenham, and many others were found in the Channel Islands. These coins are ascribed to such forgotten leaders as Cunobeline, Tasciovanus, Comux, and Tincommius.

These coins predated the conquest of Britain by the Romans. When the Romans arrived, they found the British coinage insufficient—even if they had been in the mood to accept it—and they brought with them their own coins and the same old problem: a new demand for money that stretched the mineral resources of the Empire. Even as the Romans enslaved and exploited the British tribes and dug up the British minerals, the people of the islands got back the money in coinage.

Under Hadrian, in 121, the British first used Roman coins minted in Britain, and under Carausius a separate British kingdom under Roman rule minted its own coins, of silver and bronze. One lasting feature of this Roman influence was the establishment of the lady in the flowing classical robes who would decorate British coins and stamps for centuries and be known as Britannia.

The Romans left Britain in the fifth century of the Christian era, but Roman coins and copies of them were used until the Saxon period. In 765 King Egbert minted silver pennies of his own, and these were followed by coins of Outhred and Baldred. All three varieties are scarce and expensive. More numerous were coins minted by Ethelred I, called *sceats*. The East Angles issued cop-

23

per coins and later some silver pennies. When the Vikings came to England, they added some coins, but the Saxon coins were minted through the reigns of Edward the Confessor, who came to the throne in 1042, and Harold II, who died at the battle of Hastings in 1066.

Then came the Normans, who brought with them the gold bezants of Constantinople. Yet the common coinage of Britain in this period was based on the silver penny, not on anything made of gold, because silver was fairly plentiful in Britain.

One problem in the early days of the Norman rule was the independence of the nobility. Some nobles maintained their own mints, and of these the majority succumbed to the temptation to add a pinch of this and a pinch of that to the silver, thus making more "silver" pennies with less silver. In the reign of Stephen (1135–1154) this counterfeiting by authority became a national disgrace, and almost all the earls and barons of the realm were suspected. The practice might have continued indefinitely except that the erring nobles were such bad counterfeiters. Most of these illegal coins could be discovered by simply weighing them against the legal pennies. Some of them were not even properly clipped, but were irregular in shape. There were quite enough legal mints to cause confusion —twenty-seven of them—each making coins in its own way. The king either could not remember how to spell his own name, or certain of his subjects forgot, for in his coins Stephen was spelled in various fashions, most usually "Steine." In 1141 Stephen encountered difficulties with his rebellious barons, and his wife Matilda stepped in to take command of the army while he was busy elsewhere.

The Coins of Europe

Matilda was then honored with her face on a coin. Eustace, one of their sons, struck some coins of his own. William, another son, did so too. Matilda took up arms against her husband, and the illegitimate son of Henry I commanded her armies. Naturally, all this furor was noted by the issuance of more coins.

Coins, coins, coins! They came in every size and shape. They were clipped and filed and mutilated by counterfeiters. Henry II issued some undistinguished coins. Good King Richard I and Bad King John issued few or none, but in the twelfth and early thirteenth centuries in which they reigned, the coinage of England got quite out of hand. By the middle of the twelfth century the money was so debased that citizens began to slash all coins to check their validity. Some citizens refused to accept the slashed coins as valid money. Finally, the government was forced to slash all coins so that the early money would be acceptable.

In these times the common coins showed a picture of the reigning monarch on the obverse. The reverse was dominated by a square cross. Citizens adopted the practice of chopping up the penny coins along the lines of the cross to create "halfpennies" and "fourthlings," which soon became known as farthings. This practice also served as a neat way of checking the quality of the silver inside the coin. But no one could stop there. The clipping of bits of silver from the edges of pennies became so common that a new law was passed making clipping an offense punishable by having the offender's right hand chopped off.

You can follow the improving fortunes of Britain

8 9 2 76

through its coinage. In the reign of Henry III of England the affairs of the nation prospered, and this was indicated by the beginning of gold coinage. A gold penny was introduced. It was worth 20 silver pennies. It was not very successful, however, because the merchants were not sure of the gold penny's value, and so it was withdrawn after brief circulation. During this same period the English silver penny (the *sterling*) was so valuable that men on the continent of Europe prepared counterfeits that looked just like the English pennies but were made of base metal. These were called *easterlings*. The counterfeiters made thousands of them—it was a great tribute to the prosperity of England that foreigners wanted English cloth and other goods badly enough to counterfeit the nation's money.

In the beginning of the fourteenth century in Britain, the merchants were even more prosperous. They had learned much about the outside world. Thus King Edward III was able to introduce a new gold coin, this time successfully. It was called the *noble,* and it was worth 6 shillings and 8 pence. In order to keep it worth that much and avoid the clippers, the men at the mint devised a crafty change in the process of coining. They inscribed texts from the New Testament around the *edges* of the coins. So the coin handler, by simply looking at the edges, could judge the condition of his money.

The coinage of England now began to reflect conquest and history. For over a hundred years—the official dates are from 1337 to 1453—the English tried to conquer France, in a conflict called the Hundred Years' War. During this period the English dukes who owned property in France (courtesy of their Norman ancestors) minted coins for use in that territory. The French were annoyed by seeing coins come into Paris from the regions of Gascony and Aquitaine, French territory, with English markings on them.

The warlike English were not content with fighting the French. They had no sooner slacked off their efforts to control the continent than they were involved in the Wars of the Roses, between the houses of Lancaster and York. During these fierce wars many coins were minted. The national government lost control of its coinage because the highways were not safe, and coins could not be moved from one part of the country to another. Thus each region of England depended on its local mints for coinage.

The war ended with the coming of Henry VII, first of the Tudor kings. Henry VII introduced the gold *sovereign,* another coin with writing on the edges to discourage clipping, and the silver shilling, sometimes called a *testoon.*

His successor, Henry VIII, was the most interesting monarch in all the history of coins, if in a somewhat negative way. Henry was quick to learn how to rule a kingdom. One thing he learned was that the king could make himself very rich by debasing the royal coinage. So he did just that, and earned himself the nickname "Old Coppernose" among the people.

The gold coins of England had been much respected before his day, because they were 98 percent pure gold, with just enough alloy to keep the gold from rubbing away. Henry increased the amount of alloy metal (copper) four times. Then he discovered that he could also cut down on the weight of the coins, and he did that. In 1509 the gold coin weighed 240 grains. In 1543 it weighed

27

only 200 grains, and far more of that was alloy than ever before, and two years later he cut the weight of the coin to 192 grains. Gold coins, of course, did not concern too many of the common people, but silver shillings did, and the nickname "Old Coppernose" came when Henry cut the testoon down to one-third silver and two-thirds copper. He used every known trick to debase the coinage, and his "silver" groats, at the end of his realm, were nothing more than copper coins covered with a thin coating of silver that was almost immediately rubbed off.

Henry was followed on the throne by the child king, Edward VI, who ruled only for six years, beginning when he was ten years old. When he heard the rumors around the court about the quality of the kingdom's money, he wrote in his diary that he would do something to restore the good name of the house in the land. It was time. His advisers had brought the coinage down to a level it would not touch again until after World War II. The amount of silver in the shilling was only one fourth of the total weight. The boy-king did do something—or one of his advisers did—and the shilling of 1552 was increased in silver content until it was eleven parts silver to one part alloy.

Mary Queen of Scots authorized coins including a silver half testoon. In 1976 one of these sold at auction for $5,250.

In the next few years the coinage continued to be uneven in quality, but with the coming to the throne of Henry VIII's daughter Elizabeth I, there was a new development in coinage—the introduction of machinery. A French inventor named Eloye Mestrelle devised a machine that rolled metal to the proper thickness, cut out the blanks in the proper shape of coins, and stamped them with the designs wanted. Some of these coins had corrugated edges, which helped prevent the debasement of the coins by clipping. But Mestrelle was ahead of his time. The old coinmakers set after him because he threatened their jobs, and his system made little headway. Eventually he was discharged by the royal mint. He turned to counterfeiting, and was caught, convicted, and hanged in 1578. The men with the hammers and shears went back to making coins, and a noble experiment had ended. It would be another century before the Royal Mint would adopt the processes of making coins by machinery.

Until the days of Charles I of England, there was very little change in the coinage. Oh, new coins were struck, and James I made the English accept copper coinage, although they did not like it very much. In 1576, while he was still King of Scotland only, he ordered one coin— worth £20—that sold four hundred years later for $67,500.

When Charles I came along, the resentments of the nobility against the excesses of the crown had grown very strong, and he spent almost every moment of his ill-fated reign in bitter quarreling with or fighting his own people. During the Civil War, when the troops of Parliament captured the Tower Mint and controlled most of the cities, Charles was forced to establish temporary mints and make his silver coins on the run, so to speak. Most of these pieces of silver were made from plate and other silver given to the King by his followers. They were melted down on the spot, cast into coins, and hammered, and then used to pay the troops and to buy supplies. There were many different values and sizes and shapes of these coins, and some of them were issued under state of siege, being minted inside castles while the guns boomed outside. They bore the legend OBS, short for obsidio, "siege." They showed representations of castles and walls and moats.

Some of the most rare and most interesting of these coins were issued from Beeston Castle, a fortress that was besieged until its surrender in 1645, and then was so much the object of Parliamentary anger that it was torn down stone by stone. These coins were oblong, showing a castle gateway, with the value in Roman numerals. Other pieces were issued that were round, and still others that were octagonal.

During the siege of Colchester Castle that stronghold issued several coins of irregular shape, showing a five-towered castle with the legend *Carolj fortuna resurgam* ("the fortunes of Charles shall rise again").

The coiners could not have been more mistaken. The castle fell, and so did the head of Charles I. Oliver Cromwell became protector of the realm, or dictator, and he remained in that post for five years. Then in 1660 came the restoration of the monarchy, under Charles II. His reign was marked, speaking numismatically, by the re-emergence of the figure of Britannia on the English coinage. His first Britannia coin, made in 1665, included the motto *Quattuor Maria Vindico* ("I claim the four seas"). But a few months after the coin was struck, the Dutch defeated the English in an important naval engagement, and that motto was shamefacedly chiseled off the dies,

The Coins of Europe

never to return again. The coins were valuable later. A 1675 "half dollar" brought $1,850 in 1976. The other claim to greatness of the mint in this period was the development of modern machinery to make coins, and the revival of the practice of putting inscriptions on the edges of the coins for protection against clippers. The clippers had a harder time of it in any event, because the machine coins were round, and it was hard for them to steal little bits without changing the shape of the coins.

In the seventeenth century the British government brought out the *guinea,* a gold coin that in those days was worth 20 shillings. Its name came from the place where the British secured the gold for the coins—Guinea, on the northwest coast of Africa. Later the value of the guinea was changed to 21 shillings, and still later, in 1813, the coin went out of use, although the term "guinea" was still used in the middle of the twentieth century, particularly by expensive shops and manufacturers. (There was an extra shilling in the guinea for the seller, as opposed to the twenty shillings when the price was quoted in pounds.) The abbreviation for pound, by the way—or £—comes from the Latin word *libra,* "pound." The d. that the British have always used for the abbreviation for pence, or pennies, is simply the old Latin abbreviation for denarius, because the original Saxon pennies were copies of the Roman denarii.

In 1695 the British government decided to revalue all its money, and called in all the old coins, many of which had been clipped and drilled and unmercifully abused. In charge of this operation as the master of the mint was Sir Isaac Newton, the scientist. Never was there a harder and more conscientious hunt for counterfeiters and other lawbreakers than under him. Good new coins were exchanged for bad old ones on the basis of value for value. This unexpected generosity caused Britain's government credit to soar.

In the next few years, British prosperity soared higher as England's ships raided the Spanish treasure galleons and took the bullion from the mines of South America to make British coins. Nevertheless, by the time of George III Britain had become woefully short of money and minerals suitable for coins, and so the stampover process on Spanish pieces of eight began.

After 1774, when James Watt perfected his steam engine, the use of machines made the minting of coins much easier, and coins took on a far more uniform appearance. This made it possible for the mint to produce all the coins needed, but it did not solve the metal problems. These were solved in the usual human way. The government declared that only the gold coins would contain full value of metal, and the silver coins were debased, having less than the proper amount of silver in them and depending for value on public trust in the government. After 1914, no more gold coins were minted for public circulation, either, and in later years the British were to have considerable trouble in keeping enough gold in the treasury to back their paper currency. British sovereigns, however, and British £2 gold pieces maintained a value quite their own, and were to be found throughout Europe, in places where the local currency had lost its value. This was gold—money that maintained its worth quite apart from any declarations of government.

And until the middle of the twentieth century, when

many parts of the British Empire converted from the old pounds-shillings-pence system to the metric, or dollar-and-cents, monetary systems, there were relatively few changes in British coinage. Of course, there were many oddities, produced by faulty plates and by all the usual errors to which humans are prone in manufacture. One great rarity of English coins is the 1933 penny. Only six of these were produced, it was said. Three were placed in the corner-stones of public buildings. Three made their way into museums. But if anyone anywhere should find a seventh 1933 English penny, he is likely to become a very wealthy man.

2. The Continent

Charlemagne had attempted to build a Holy Roman Empire, which would unify all of Christian Europe. It was a brave dream, but little more, because when Charlemagne died, so did his empire. The Germans, for their part, broke away into little dukedoms and kingdoms, which maintained their own armies, courts, and currencies. This has created a field day for coin collectors.

At first those coins modeled on the Roman denarii were used almost everywhere, and they were copied with crude imitations. By about 1100 the Germans in various city-states were making coins which would later be called *bractea,* Latin for "thin sheet of metal," because they were minted out of metal so thin that they were stamped only on one side and the design showed through the other. They were debased, for the most part, and fell quickly out of use.

Frederick Barbarossa and his grandson Frederick II tried to make a true empire out of Germany and attach Italy to it, but they did not succeed. Until the day in 1871 when Wilhelm I was proclaimed Emperor of Germany, there was no German nation, but a loose grouping of individual states. Thus there are hundreds of different "German" coins. During this period, what we now call Germany and Austria were divided into 350 duchies and kingdoms, so the collector who tries to specialize in German states has picked himself a good-sized job.

Frederick II issued a handsome coin called an *augustal,* which was regarded as the finest of the continental medieval coins. Lübeck issued silver *thalers.* So did Cologne. Nürnberg put out *ducats.* Lüneburg, which housed a famous astronomical observatory, showed a picture of the man in the moon on the reverse of its silver thalers.

But as time went on, some order came out of this chaos. The richer cities, such as Cologne, Mainz, Frankfurt, and Nürnberg, issued gold coins based on the Florentine gold *florin.* (Florence was then one of the powers of the world, for this was the period of the Renaissance in Italy.) The unity among these cities was brought about by the Catholic Church, which held much property and was very strong in all Europe. The archbishops agreed among themselves to the values in the coins.

But as time went on, and the gold from the German mines was harder to find, the usual debasement set in, and silver coins became more important. By 1500 a standard silver coin was struck at Joachimsthal in Bohemia. It was called the *joachimsthaler,* and it became the most popular of Germanic coins, copied all over the world. It was the model for the piece of eight, for the American dollar, and for the Austrian *Maria Theresa thalers* that would dominate Africa and the Middle East in the years to come.

This Austrian power began with a Swiss family, the Hapsburgs. Rudolf I Hapsburg was elected Holy Roman Emperor in 1273, and the family fortunes began to rise. After 1438 all the Holy Roman Emperors were Hapsburgs. Behind this throne stood the banking family of Fugger, which owned silver mines in the Tyrol and Carinthia and gold mines in Hungary and Bohemia. At one time the Fuggers cornered the German market in copper, and when the Hapsburgs married into the ruling family of Spain, the Fuggers took over the Spanish mercury mines. So important was banking and money that soon Jacob Fugger had an interesting nickname—*Rex denariorum,* "Money King." In 1740, there came to the throne of the Hapsburgs a princess, Maria Theresa, under whose reign were issued the most famous coins in all the world, those Maria Theresa thalers.

The original Maria Theresa thalers were issued in 1780, and thereafter millions of them were coined. Some were coined by the Hapsburgs, until their dynasty fell at the end of World War I. Afterward mints at Brussels, London, Bombay, and San Francisco continued to make Maria Theresa thalers. All of these—even thalers coined by Mussolini in 1935 after he captured Ethiopia—still bore the magic date 1780. The reason is simple enough. The people of the Middle East and Africa accepted this coin in trade because it was big and heavy, and its regal design and powerful-looking seal on the reverse gave a feeling of authority and value. Since the original coins were dated 1780, primitive people would accept no others. A few were coined elsewhere with different dates, but they were never successful.

Although the British experimented with coins after the Romans left the islands, it was natural, with the heritage of Rome, that the Italian peninsula would emerge as the place where the art of coinage was perfected. The Renaissance of art and literature began there, and with it came fine designs for coins and standardization of coins. The Florentine florin, for example, was known across Europe for the design and the purity of its content, and this was coined as early as 1252. Among the great artists of the Italian peninsula, and the world, were Benvenuto Cellini and Leonardo da Vinci. Both of these men designed coins. The first efficient machinery for making coins was developed by Donato Bramante, an architect, around 1500, and Leonardo, with his draftsman's eye and engineer's mind, improved greatly on this. Cellini designed a number of gold coins for several Popes.

Among the famous coins of Europe is one Dutch coin, the *Leyden thaler,* which was struck to commemorate the deliverance of the city of Leyden from the Spanish, who had besieged it for many months, forcing the people into starvation so severe that they were glad to eat rats and mice. The thaler shows King Sennacherib's force melting away before the gates of Jerusalem, and the comparison is obvious.

Another famous coin is Amsterdam's *trade dollar,* which was first coined in 1601 as a symbol of the progress and hopes of the great Dutch trading companies that were then moving around the world, to the East and West Indies and along the Hudson River of North America. The coin was struck just a year before formation of the East India company, which established the Dutch colonies in what is now Indonesia, and earned excellent profits for two hundred years. Then came the West Indies company, which was so prosperous in the beginning that the British declared a trade war against the Netherlands that lasted several decades.

During the Dark Ages of Europe the coins of the Byzantine emperors at Constantinople were much in use in northern Europe, for a very interesting reason. The Vikings wandered the earth, and many of them served in the Byzantine armies as soldiers and sailors.

In Scandinavia, in recent years, some fifty thousand Byzantine coins have been unearthed. Until the end of the fourteenth century the three Scandinavian nations of Denmark, Norway, and Sweden were totally independent, but in 1397 they formed what was known as the Union of Kalmar. This brought about a common device—the three crowns that one sees on Danish coins, Swedish coins, and in many public places in the northern countries.

Denmark was the original leader of this union, but eventually Sweden took over as principal nation of Scandinavia and moved afield in attempts to become a world power, even sending emissaries to colonize in the New World, in what is now Delaware. This ended with the career of Charles XII, who impoverished his nation with his military excesses. Baron de Goertz, one of his advisers, suggested what seemed to be an admirable and simple way to replenishing the wasted Swedish treasury.

All the government had to do, he said, was call in the silver coins and put the silver in the treasury. In exchange, the people would receive copper coins cut from the same dies, and these, by law, would be declared to have the same value. It was a very easy way out, said the baron. And so it was done—the currency was depreciated. But the people of Sweden rose up so rebelliously that the King arrested the baron. He was tried and beheaded for his bright idea.

Poland contributed one of the most rare and celebrated of all European coins. It is the *100-ducat gold piece* coined in 1621 during the reign of Sigismund III. Also notable for some of its coins is Russia, where the *ruble* originated sometime during the eighth century of the Christian era. The ruble was not a circular coin to begin with, but was shaped like a diamond with flat ends. It was called a *griuna* originally, which meant "bag money," and that name was given the coin because it resembled a horsehide bag commonly used in Russia then. This money was made of iron, and it was very valuable at the time, because iron was scarce and useful.

Sweden developed an even stranger kind of money in later years, using plates of copper, some of them two feet long and a foot wide and weighing more than forty pounds. They were worth the equivalent of $150. It was not possible to cover the whole surface with a design, so coins were stamped into the metal at the four ends and in the middle to keep clippers from going to work on the slabs. In these northern countries, strange money was not at all unusual. A few years after Queen Christina of Sweden had sanctioned the slab currency, Peter the Great of Russia ordered the stamping of small copper coins that showed on the reverse side a picture of a nose, mouth, moustache, and beard. These were called *beard tokens*. They were designed as coins of receipt for a special tax. Peter went to western Europe as a young man in the 1690's, and noticed that many of the people of the west —the vast majority—were clean shaven and wore modern clothes. So when he came back to Russia in 1698, he decided that his people should shave off their beards. Peter issued many other drastic orders, but none so offended the Russian people as the order to shave their beards. If God had not intended men to have beards, they said, quite logically, then why did He allow whiskers to grow on their faces? Even an absolute monarch, even in Russia, was subject to some forms of public opinion, and Peter backed down on the beard issue—at least partly. He announced that his subjects could keep their beards if they would pay a special beard tax, and thus were minted the beard tokens that would show that the bearded ones had paid their taxes.

Peter was very much impressed with the French, because he came to the west at the time the French were enjoying their greatest prestige, during the reign of Louis XIV, known as the Sun King. Louis was a great spender and left his kingdom very poor. His great-grandson, Louis XV, was even more a spender, and *his* grandson, Louis XVI, was not only married to the extravagant Marie Antoinette, but recklessly helped to finance the American Revolution. The bankruptcy of the French kingdom certainly helped bring about the French revolution.

When the revolution came in the late 1780's, the government could not even borrow money from its citizens. They were burying all their coins in the ground. In

November, 1789, the French Parliament confiscated all the property of the Roman Catholic Church in France and, because there was so little metal for coinage, issued paper bills called *assignats,* in the amount of 400 millon livres, a huge sum, which enabled the people to purchase these confiscated properties. Within one year France had three times as much paper money in circulation, and the money problem had become so acute that even the government printers who made the money did not believe in it. They went on strike until they were promised a loaf of bread each day instead of paper money. The value of the assignats dropped to less than 10 percent of the face amount, and finally went down to less than 1 percent of face value. The problem was only solved in 1796 when Napoleon, the conqueror, invaded Italy and "requisitioned" millions of Italian coins of gold and silver. At one point he even raided the Vatican's coin collection. Napoleon was notable in that, while he was doing this, he was also telling the Italians that he had relieved them of their chains and liberated them from slavery. A few days after he made that statement, he took millions of coins away from the people of Milan in order to send them back to France.

Napoleon came home from his wars of conquest and strengthened his power by putting the French money back on its feet. He devised a 5-franc silver piece and introduced the decimal system of coinage. That 5-franc piece was worth about a dollar, and it was about the same size as the Maria Theresa coin and the Spanish piece of eight.

3
The Coins of Asia

In China in the sixth century, a gentleman named Liu Ch'ien made a catalog of the coins issued by the Imperial government—as a matter of record, not for collectors. We only know about this catalog because it is mentioned in other writings, for the catalog itself was lost a few years later. The next Chinese coin cataloger was a noble named Ku Hsuan, who put together a series of records of coins a few years later. These, too, were lost. Then came a succession of other records. The only trouble with their findings was that in those old days the numismatists depended largely on mythology for their information, and so some of their facts were very farfetched. This is true of much of Chinese cultural history, and it accounts for the conflicting claims heard so often about inventions common to East and West.

The fact, as established by modern Chinese coin experts, is that ancient Chinese copper coins date back to about the seventh century before the birth of Christ. This dating matches up generally with the coming of coins to the Western world.

In the beginning of their history, the Chinese suffered several difficulties in the matter of creating money. Neither gold nor silver was produced within the old Shang and Chou kingdoms. Cowrie shells, copper, and bronze were available, and so this is how Chinese coins developed.

One would scarcely even call them coins in the modern sense. Cowrie and clam shells served as money, for ornaments, and as utensils for digging and eating. Not only did the Chinese use cowrie shells for money, they also used imitation cowrie shells.

In the twelfth century B.C. the Chinese had another form of money. It was called *I Pi Ch'ien,* or ant-nose money, and it was something like cowrie shells, only made of bronze. In 1936 in Anhui Province, archaeologists found 130 pieces of this money stuck together in a huge mass.

These pieces of ant-nose money and the cowrie shells were not truly coins, but the next form of Chinese money was coined. This was the *spade* coinage, named because of the shape of these early coins, which date back to the 8th century B.C. They were small bronze copies of spades and other farm implements, which had formerly been used for barter. The spade coins were extremely valuable, and they were used to trade for silk and other expensive items. Next came the *knife* coins, which were modeled after real knives. They were issued by various rulers in different sizes and denominations, and were used in the period around 300 B.C.

The Coins of Asia

Real coins of gold, bearing stamp marks and apparently made in about the same way as the Greek stater, were used in the kingdom of Ch'u about two hundred years before the birth of Christ. They were called *yuan chin.* Not all were made of gold. Some of copper and some of lead have been found, and even a few of silver. Another kind of "money," made of yellow clay, was stamped to look like the gold money. Chinese historians believe this was funeral money, created to look like real money but made of substances of little value.

About the middle of the 3rd century B.C., the Chinese invented or discovered the round shape for coins. The knife coins had been made with large round holes on the ends so they could be strung together on a rope for easy carrying. The round coins were made with holes in the center, so they, too, could be strung together.

In the days of the feudal Chinese states, the king and his nobles all coined money as they needed it, for the metal in the money was the guarantee of its value. But when the many warring states were unified under the Ch'in dynasty in 221 B.C., Emperor Shih Huang Ti replaced all forms of money then in use by the issue of round coins weighing half an ounce, thus creating a uniform currency.

The Chinese also used gold cubes for money and pieces of silver cast in the shape of shoes. The bronze and copper pieces with holes in them, called *cash,* were in use in China for hundreds of years. Also, in modern times, after the influence of the Spanish and other European adventurers was felt in Asia, the Chinese turned to the use of the piece of eight and later to the Mexican dollar, which was roughly the same size and weight. The Spanish were introduced into China in the sixteenth century from the Philippines, by then a Spanish colony. Later, when China became a republic, Chinese silver dollars were also coined. These supplemented but did not replace the Mexican dollars.

Before 1875 the only official "money" in coins was the cash. It was not a very valuable coin. Then the Chinese dollar was issued, bearing a bust of the god of longevity on one side and Chinese characters on the other. Its value was 7 *mace* and 2 *candareens*. (Mace and candareens were equivalent to one tenth and one one hundreth, respectively, of China's basic unit of weight, the *toll*.) Much interesting money in coins was issued after the revolution of 1911, from a 1912 dollar showing President Yuan Shi-kai, to a 1928 dollar showing a picture of an automobile in Kweichow Province. (The latter, in the 1970's, was one of the most valued of modern Chinese coins.)

After about 700 A.D., the Japanese used the Chinese system of square-holed cash, until the middle of the nineteenth century. Then a modern system of coinage was established in Japan based on the *yen,* which was a silver coin about the size of a dollar. In fact, the Japanese coined a trade dollar, which contained 420 grains of silver. It was a good coin, and in the 1970's was valued highly.

Coins had been invented, apparently quite independently, in the civilization of India, before the coming of Alexander the Great to that subcontinent. One Indian king paid a tribute to Alexander and the Macedonian armies of eighty talents of coined silver. This was made up of punch-marked silver coins, far superior in workmanship to the early coinage of the Greeks. The Westerners discovered then that many Indian princes and kings minted their own coins of gold and silver. The most famous of these was the great Emperor of the Moguls, Shah Jehan, who ruled in Delhi in 1628. Under his reign were minted the valuable and beautiful gold *mohurs,* intricately designed coins that have become very valuable. One tale of Indian coinage involves the minting of the *Kashmiri rupee* in 1846 by the Muslim ruler Gulab Singh:

One day Gulab Singh was talking to the British resident in Kashmir, Sir Henry Lawrence.

"Lawrence Sahib, why is it that in the end the English always conquer, even though at first all goes against them?" he asked.

The resident reached for a piece of paper and wrote the letters IHS. This is the symbol for the name of Jesus, and it has often appeared on coins minted in Christian countries.

Gulab Singh did not understand the meaning of the letters, and he did not ask. Instead, he pondered long over them, and decided that they represented some special magic of the British. He decided to take a leaf from their book. So the next coins of Kashmir bore the symbols IHS—as no other coins in the Muslim world have ever done, before or since.

4
Odd Kinds of Money

There is a legitimate part of numismatics that has nothing to do with coins and currency, and this involves pieces—strange symbols of exchange that were once used as money.

In Ancient Egypt around 2000 B.C., the people were coming out of the rudimentary civilization of village and farm and moving into cities, where many people specialized in only one variety of work. When a man spent all his time making pottery, he found it difficult to exchange his goods for all the materials he needed, or to do so exactly and at the time that he wished. So there grew up certain practices of trading for items that everyone would want. Chief among these in Egypt was a sack of grain of a certain weight, because everyone used grain to make flour. The trouble with grain, however, was that it could be eaten by rats, or spoiled by water, or decayed by the sun. A better trading material was linen. Everyone used linen in making the clothes of Egypt. Yet linen also could be ruined by fire, dirt, or water.

When the Egyptians discovered gold and other scarce metals, they began to use bowls and other standard implements made of these precious metals for trade. They found that copper was the common cheap metal, and silver was worth forty times as much. Gold was worth twice as much as silver.

By about 1600 B.C. the use of bowls in Egypt had proved a little taxing, and so money rings were developed. These were not yet coins, but they were quite close to the idea of coinage. The rings could be worn on arms or fingers and could be carried in strings, bound together by strips of papyrus.

Now many other countries developed moneys of their own that predated or lived along with coins. In Siam, the first moneys were small gold and silver pieces shaped like bullets. These were made according to weight, based on the *tical,* and these pieces were in use right up until 1904, when they were declared illegal. The Siamese also had coins that were shaped like packsaddles for horses, and others made of porcelain, and still others that, like Chinese coins, were made from pure tin. The Malayans used tin pieces that were cast in molds and were decorated with designs and writing. The people of Malacca used lead pieces shaped like roosters.

Among the islanders of the Pacific, many kinds of money were taken from the sea. Some bracelets of shark's teeth were used as money. The Fijians made money of whales' teeth. The people of the Solomon Islands made money of coconut shells. In New Guinea, mother-of-pearl was cut into round disks, holes were cut in the middle, and the disks were made into bracelets that passed as money. Dogs were scarce in New Guinea, so the New Guinea tribes used dogs' teeth for money. Then Chinese traders brought in hundreds of dogs from the mainland of China, thus debasing the New Guinea tribal currency. German traders made things even worse by bringing in artificial dogs' teeth, and so tooth currency came to an end there.

The Samoans used finely made mats for currency, and the people of Yap in the Caroline Islands used the largest and most impressive currency in the world—huge stone disks, some of them twelve feet in diameter. The stones came from the island of Peleliu, four hundred miles away. The stones had to be quarried and then brought to Yap by canoe and raft. A stone about two feet across, weighing fifty pounds, would buy a thousand coconuts, and two such stones would buy a wife.

In Africa for a long time cowrie shells were used as money, and until quite recently these shells were currency along the Niger River. In other parts of Africa, as long as the white man dominated the continent, glass beads were used as money. Four hundred different kinds and colors came into existence there, strung on palm fiber. A beaded thread reaching from the tip of the index finger to the wrist was known as a *bitil*. Four bitils made a *khete* and 10 khete made a *fundo*. Copper wire was also used by the natives as money, and so were spades, bells, and bars— quite reminiscent of ancient China.

A quarter of a century ago, money in Africa was unbelievably crude. In Liberia certain tribes supported themselves by mining iron ore, fashioning it into pieces about as thick as a lead pencil and several feet in length, with one end flattened into the shape of a wing and the other into a double tail. This was called a *gizi penny,* and it passed as money. It was worth about 2 American cents, or, in 1940, enough rice to last one person a week.

The Miyanda tribe made iron rings, which passed as money and also as jewelry. The Kanakas made spearheads, which were money and weapons. Iron hoes were money in the Sudan, and bundles of tiny iron knives were used as money in the Gaboon area of French Equatorial Africa. In the Congo, "money" was made from the hairs of elephants' tails, zebras' tails, and giraffes' tails. In the Gold Coast the natives used copper rings, in the French Guinea region, amber beads were money, and in Angola strips of mat made of rice straw were money. The natives of the Bamboon district of French Cameroons used a brass coin that looked like a frog. In Ethiopia a brass gun cartridge could be money.

Before anyone scoffs at these many strange forms of money, let him recall that in America in the early days of settlement beaver skins were used by the Hudson's Bay Company as money, and in Massachusetts Bay Colony, musket bullets were given the value of farthings, and that everywhere along the East Coast wampum was used as money. In fact, both the Indians and the whites even *counterfeited* wampum. How did they do it? Well, there were two kinds of wampum, one made from the blue eye of the quahog clam shell and one made from the white periwinkle shell. These pieces were strung on threads like beads. The quahog wampum was worth twice as much as the periwinkle wampum, so the counterfeiters dyed the white beads bluish black, thus doubling their value. In 1650 the council of the Dutch colony of New Netherlands had this to say:

> We have by experience and for a long time seen the decline and daily depreciation of the loose Wampum, among which are circulating many without holes and half finished, also some of Stone, Bone, Glass Muscle Shells, yea even of Wood and Broken Beads.

Matters became so serious that a dozen years later wampum was outlawed in Massachusetts, but only because too many people were counterfeiting it.

5
The Coins
of the Americas

Long before any but a handful of Englishmen were trying to scrape a foothold on the eastern American coast at Jamestown, mints were pouring forth millions of coins at Mexico City and points farther south. The original coins were made at the Mexico mint, which was established by Spanish royal decree in 1535. Copper was used at first, but no one had any faith in copper, and the coins were so ugly and badly struck that the Indians threw 200,000 of them into the waters of Lake Texcoco. The Spanish then made silver coins from pieces of hammered silver, which had been struck with a die and then cut out with shears. Altogether, probably a billion pieces of eight, which represented eight Spanish *reales,* were produced at the Mexico City mint. Since there were three other important mints in Spanish America, all producing at about the same rate, that gives an indication of the amount of money made by Spain. Indeed, during the sixteenth and seventeenth centuries, Spain made more money than any other nation in the world.

The American dollar was modeled on the piece of eight, but it was not to come for a long time. The first money used in the English colonies—and the French and Dutch also, for that matter—was the money of the home country. Only a few coins were struck in North America by separate colonies, until the opening of the United States Federal Mint in 1792. This mint was located at Philadelphia, the early seat of American government, and it was to remain there always. Other mints would be established and abandoned, but the chief American mint would be in Philadelphia, and the coins made there would be the only ones that did not carry a small initial letter (called a mintmark).

But even while the American government was issuing money, the Spanish dollars, or pieces of eight, were considered to be legal tender in the United States.

Among the most valuable of American coins are some rarities issued by the various colonies. Massachusetts was the first, if one disregards the shilling and lesser coins issued in England for use of the Virginia Company. These were used almost entirely in Bermuda, anyhow. In 1652 Massachusetts Bay Colony issued a primitive shilling, with the initials *N.E.* for "New England" on one side, and the value in pence in Roman numerals on the other side. And then began the most active counterfeiting, considering the number of people involved as opposed to the number of total citizens, that the world has ever known. It started with clippers, who nicked and gouged and pounded off pieces of the coins, and then sold the silver. Consequently, whole or even reasonably whole shillings became very rare, and the value rose until by the middle of the twentieth century, such shillings sold for as much as $500 at auction. Lesser coins, the New England sixpence and the New England threepenny bit, were even rarer and more expensive.

The New England shilling was issued for only about five months. Because it was so easy to deface, the governor of Massachusetts colony decided to issue better money, and the *pine tree shillings* came into use. (These were actually willow tree, oak tree, and finally pine tree coins.) This shilling brought a fortune for one man—John Hull, the coiner and silversmith. He received a fee of 15 pence for every 20 shillings minted, and he became so wealthy that, when he died in 1683, he left his daughter £30,000.

Although England was very jealous of the right of coinage, the colonies had to have coins, and so one government after another took up the process. So did private coiners, of whom John Higley, owner of a copper mine at Granby, Connecticut, was one of the first. Early in the eighteenth century he made coins that he stamped with the words "Value of Threepence." Since these were not backed by any government, many people did not believe they were worth 3 pence, and the value fluctuated. Still, there was a demand. Higley solved his problem by issuing new 3-pence coins. On one side they said, "I Am Pure Copper." On the other side they said, "Value Me As You Please." The people did, and everyone was satisfied. John Higley's copper mine continued in operation.

Higley's coins were called tokens, because they had no

official backing, and in the colonies there was such need that many tokens were issued for the making of small change. In Virginia and elsewhere, tobacco was used as money, and notes of exchange were issued on the basis of it, each one carrying the value of the hogsheads that backed it. Tobacco notes were legal tender up until the Revolution. There were many kinds of tokens, from a brass New York token, issued by the Dutch, which represents either Venus or an Indian squaw (nobody could tell which) and the Saint Patrick money of New Jersey, which shows King David playing a harp, and is inscribed in faulty Latin (*Quiescat Plebs* for "Let the People Be Still").

When the revolutionaries of the New World rebelled against England, they needed coins (and paper money, too, which will be described later), and they issued Continental money. One piece of this was the Continental dollar. Continental dollars were made at Philadelphia, in London, and in Birmingham. On one side the coin said "Continental Currency 1776. Mind Your Business." On the other side it showed thirteen chain links representing the North American but not Canadian colonies. "We Are One," said the legend.

These coins were made of pewter, silver, and sometimes of brass, depending on the need and the materials available. The most valuable are the 1776 silver dollar that says "Currency" with two *r*'s, and the brass piece that says "Curency" with one *r,* and the silver piece that says *E. G. Fecit* ("E. G. made it"). As to the many other coins of the Continental series, they were worth somewhere between $75 and $200 in the 1970's, depending on condition.

Condition is everything in coin collecting. If someone is lucky enough to find a new coin that has never been passed around, or circulated, it can be worth ten times as much as an exact replica that has been hard used as money and whose inscriptions are worn away or whose edges have been filed or clipped. In coins—far more than in stamps, for example—the condition is very important in determining the value. One reason for this, of course, is that coins do not perish as easily as stamps or currency. They are inclined to be among the most durable of man's possessions. That is why it is still possible to collect ancient Greek and Roman coins without being a millionaire, but it is also a good reason for the huge differences in the value of the same coins.

Even during the Revolutionary War, the currency of the Continental Congress fluctuated in value very markedly, and much property was lost. For example, the mother of Commodore Vanderbilt suffered from this when all her family's fortune was invested in Continental money in a outburst of patriotism, and this money deteriorated from the moment it was made. She lost everything. Before the war was well along, the shortage of money was so great, too, that the coiners were making pennies out of the buttons of the Continental soldier's uniforms, and the soldiers were selling off their buttons. One of these button pennies in the 1970's was worth $75.

The confusion that existed at the end of the Revolutionary War provided a field day for later collectors, because most of the states or people in those states issued some kind of money. The federal government issued money. (One 1794 Washington copper half-dollar was worth about $900 in the 1970's.) Most interesting was the money issued by the Republic of Vermont, which was left out of the original thirteen states and had to go it alone for a time. So as an independent nation Vermont issued her own money.

Among the various states so much small money was issued that it is not particularly rare even in the last half of the twentieth century, and thus not particularly valuable in many cases.

At that time the American financier Robert Morris attempted to reform the whole idea of money and to adopt the decimal system. He drew plans for money based on a 1,000-unit piece called a *mark,* with a 500-unit piece called a *quint,* and a 100-unit piece called a *bit.* A coin based on these designs (although the system was ignored) came out called the *Nova Constellatio* ("New Constellation") copper cent, some of which were stamped from dies in which *Constellatio* was spelled *Constelatio.* The cents with the error became very valuable for a while, until it was discovered that there was just about as large a supply of the errors as there was of the originals.

In this period was coined one of the most valuable of all American pieces, the *Brasher doubloon.* This coin is named for Ephraim Brasher, a New York goldsmith. Brasher was particularly notable in his day for his efforts to establish a mint in New York State, if only one to make copper cents. (The new states needed coins so badly that they were importing thousands every month from England.) Brasher petitioned the legislature for the right to make coins, and nothing happened, but a mint was established in Newburgh and continued until 1791. Brasher did not make small coins then, but he did coin several large gold pieces in 1787. About a half dozen of these survived into the middle of the twentieth century, when two were known to be in private hands. They were valued at around $10,000 each, although one of them was insured for $100,000. What were they worth? It was, as with any valuable, a matter of supply and demand and the desire of any wealthy collector at any given time to sell or auction. All one could say was that the Brasher doubloon was very rare and thus very valuable.

The United States Mint was established in 1792, but not so very many coins were issued by the American government in its early years. In the first fifty-six years of American coinage—from 1792 until 1848—the United States mints struck 343 million pieces. This sounds like quite a large number, yet in one year in the late 1950's, the mints produced 2 billion pieces of money for circulation, to say nothing of 3 billion proofs for collectors and other purposes. Since that time production has continued at a high rate.

Alexander Hamilton, first American Secretary of the Treasury, had some interesting ideas about money. He insisted on creating a half-cent coin. His idea was that such a small coin would help the poor of America by keeping shopkeepers from raising prices. If a loaf of bread, for example, sold for 3 cents and the customer wanted only half a loaf, he was forced to pay 2 cents, or two thirds of the price for the loaf. But with a half-cent coin, he could pay exactly half the price.

So the half-cent coins were minted. They failed, because the shopkeepers detested this small coin, which made their lives miserable and cut into their profits. The people, poor and otherwise, did not rise up to protect the coinage, and soon the shopkeepers were refusing to accept half cents.

Four types of half cents were made between 1793 and 1857, but they never caught on as part of the American monetary system, and they were never made legal tender, which would have forced storekeepers to accept them in payment of debts. In 1793 about 32,000 of them were made, and in the 1960's one of these in very fine condition was worth about $300. But most of the others developed far less value, because so many were made. One type of 1797 with a lettered edge came to be worth about $350, one of 1811 came to be worth about $300, although 115,000 of them were minted. And, of course, even the most common half cents in only fair condition had some value. By the middle of the twentieth century, even the worst and most common were worth at least two or three dollars.

Another common coin of America was the large penny piece, of which 150 million were minted altogether between 1793 and 1857, when the mint stopped coining so large a piece. Yet the number of coins that survived was nothing like this, because copper came to be scarce in America for a time, and manufacturers would go to the banks, buy kegs of pennies, and melt them down for their metal content. Consequently, some large copper pennies, or one-cent pieces, reached a value of $650–750, although a million of them were made. This was true of the issues of 1799, in particular, and many of the other pennies were found to be worth hundreds of dollars if they were in very fine or uncirculated condition.

The Coins of the Americas

In 1856 the mint authorities cut down the size of the American penny to about the size of the one used in the 1970's. This saved a considerable amount of copper, for one thing. That year the decision was made to cut down the coinage before the authorizing legislation was passed by Congress, and a thousand pennies were issued. (Some say that these were not legal coins because they had not been authorized. As far as collectors were concerned, that was just fine. The pennies were worth between $350 and $2,000 in the 1970's.)

But good values remained in these coins. Even after forty million of them were struck, the 1857s and 1858s were worth as much as $400. One of the problems for the collector of coins—far more than for the collector of stamps—was to be sure he was not cheated. In the pennies of 1856–1858, for example, there was much shaving and altering of the 1858s to make them appear to be of the rarer 1856 variety, and one can see why: The value was about five times as great.

The famous American *Indian head penny* was brought into use in 1858, although not very many pieces were made (about a hundred in all). Many billions of these were minted between 1859 and 1909, but they remained valuable—in the sense that even the most common and worthless of them still would bring a good price in the 1970's, and the best of them would bring a hundred or two hundred dollars, with the exception of the 1869 or 1868 issue, which in proof condition was yet unknown, and the 1864 with an L on the ribbon, which was called rare—and that meant that it would bring whatever the seller could get.

Coins, Collectors and Counterfeiters

The more modern coins tend to be less valuable, because so many more of them were issued as the United States grew in population. There are exceptions, even among the lowly pennies. The 1922 *Lincoln head cent* with no *D* on it is very valuable today. So is a 1955 Lincoln penny of the new design, with an error—a doubled die on the front or obverse side.

Then consider the 1913 *Liberty head nickel*. Only five are known to exist, and one sold recently for $46,000.

There are so many varieties, years of issue, errors, and specialties that a catalog is needed by anyone really interested in coins, either as a speculator or a collector. Plenty of both breeds live in America.

6
The Collectors

The collection of coins is a relatively modern development, for the same reason that collection of art and other objects of value is too.

For many centuries after the fall of Rome, there was very little interest in ancient civilizations or practices. To be sure, the old marble statues of the Greeks and Romans were dug up. Many times they were defaced and the marble used again for other purposes. So it was with the coinage and wealth of the ancients—the coins were often melted down for the metal, which was then made into modern coins of the period or into jewelry. Or sometimes the ancient coins were simply hoarded for their value and circulated as money when coins were short.

Coin collecting demanded two conditions: a large supply of coins in existence and the leisure and wealth of a class that could afford to save coins rather than spend them and had the time to compare and enjoy the study of coins.

At first only kings, nobles, and the princes of the church had such wealth and such leisure.

In the seventeenth century the Convent of Saint Florian purchased the coin collection of a Venetian poet named Apostolo Zeno. This purchase predated the general rise in collecting by many years, but the first indications of an interest in coins go back much further. In 1489 Angelo Poliziano, a friend of Lorenzo de' Medici, published what is believed to be the very first work on coins. It dealt with the coins of the ancient world. Among the coin collections of the world, the Vatican's will always be a leader, for it was begun very early, and many powerful rulers contributed heavily to it. In the 1950's that collection was said to number more than a hundred thousand items.

The necessary conditions were met in England when the Industrial Revolution of the mid-eighteenth century created a wealthy middle class. By 1790 many provincial small coins were in circulation as well as British government coins. At that time a man named James Conder brought out a catalog of small coins called *An Arrangement of Provincial Coins, Tokens, and Medalets*. This guide was invaluable in the detection of counterfeits, for perhaps a quarter of the privately made coins on the market were legitimate, and three quarters of these new coins were counterfeits. Many in Britain then saved the Spanish dollars, which were minted from silver found in the New World. Sometimes the silver dollars were countermarked over the Spanish design with a bust of King George III.

Although these silver coins were not terribly valuable,

and the privately made copper coins were even less so, gentlemen of the realm took to collecting them as a hobby, separating them by the various groups, known as *varieties,* which indicated their place of coinage. There were even varieties of counterfeits.

A number of newspapers and magazines began to carry information about the wide range of coins available, and this again increased interest in the hobby. Soon a guidebook to coins, called *The Virtuoso's Companion,* was issued by an enterprising British publisher, and this spread the hobby even further. By the end of the century, it was estimated that several thousand British gentlemen spent much of their spare time in the identification and handling of coins. This particular fad, in England, subsided around the turn of the nineteenth century, but by that time a definite hobby had been established. Several dealers in London specialized in the gathering and selling of coins.

At this time, there was very little interest in coins anywhere else in the world. Most governments did not save their own coins. The dies and other items used in manufacture were destroyed when they had ceased to be useful. In 1793 the United States Mint in Philadelphia issued its first coins—cents and half cents. The next year the mint issued a half dime, half dollar, and silver dollar, and in 1796 the dime and quarter were added, but the American government did not save specimens, and very few Americans (about two dozen in all) were interested in coin collecting. So the finest of these coins to be saved were sent over to England, where they were preserved in excellent condition by British coin collectors. It was nearly a half century later that Americans became interested in saving coins for collecting purposes. When these Americans did become interested, they found that the place to find early American coins was England, partly because of the circumstances mentioned, and partly because the original colonial coins, even those struck for use exclusively in North America, were at first manufactured in England.

Coin collecting very soon became the art of identifying and isolating differences among coins. In the coin book published by Conder, so many different varieties were produced by different governments that there was a real challenge in collecting these bits of small silver and copper. And after coins were put into wide use in England, these British coins were also brought to the colonies to relieve a coin shortage—so further confusions set in, all of which brought great joy to collectors. It was not much of a change then for gentlemen interested in coins to branch out. (It was considered most unladylike for a woman to take an interest in so vulgar a commodity as money, and so the ladies were not encouraged to join the men.)

Coin collecting in this period had some political overtones, too. Many who did not like the government's policy made their feelings known through conversation about coins. In 1770, when the first halfpenny piece with the image of George III appeared, a coin collector named Pinkerton had this to say: "The first halfpence present such a face as human being never wore, jutting out something in the likeness of a macaw."

The Royal Mint brought in thousands of Spanish pieces of eight from the mints at Mexico City, Lima, Peru, and Potosi, Bolivia. These were stamped with the figure of

Charles IV of Spain. The English then stamped these Spanish coins with an image of George III. Another coin collector had this to say:

> The Bank, to make their Spanish dollar pass
> Stamped the head of a fool on the head of an Ass.

One of the earliest coin dealers in the world was Mayer Amschel Rothschild, a child of the ghetto of Frankfurt, who worked for several years in the Oppenheimer banking house in Hamburg. When Rothschild was a very young man, standing behind the counter in the Oppenheimer house, he handled hundreds of foreign coins from far-off lands. He became interested in the coins themselves as much as for their value as money. When Rothschild was twenty years old, he returned to Frankfurt and set himself up in the coin business. The trouble was that he could not find enough collectors to make a living. So he was also a sort of pawnbroker. Yet he persisted in printing catalogs of European coins and trying to make a go of it.

One day Rothschild met a fellow coin enthusiast he had known in Hamburg, who was now attached to the court of Prince William of Hesse. This courtier brought some members of the court of William to the coin shop. Rothschild explained the mysteries of coins. The members of the court were intrigued by this new pastime, and it was not too long before Rothschild's coin business increased. He was careful in his designation of coins and in seeing that those he handled had not been clipped or drilled so that their value was diminished. He used a guide called the *Vollständiges Thaler Cabinet,* which was then the best

German coin catalog available. This catalog listed the country, date, and serial number (as established by the catalogers) of each German coin. It did not say anything about condition—that was part of the gamble of collecting. Even in the second half of the twentieth century, coin collectors do well to watch the condition of anything they buy, for the old ways are hard to change.

Rothschild was wise enough to handle only excellent coins, and one day when he was not expecting anything in particular, this habit stood him in very good stead. He had gone to the palace to sell coins to some of his acquaintances—and suddenly he was ushered into the presence of Prince William, who had heard of this new hobby. Fortunately, Rothschild had a good sampling with him, and his wares and manner made a favorable impression on the prince. He sold Prince William some coins at about twice their face value, which gave the dealer a good profit and yet was not exorbitant.

Soon William became a regular customer. With royal backing, the hobby became ever more popular in Frankfurt, and Rothschild opened a banking business on a small scale in order to supply his coin business with material. He sold coins to the wealthy nobles, who took up this diversion with the approval of their prince. Rothschild's coin business increased, Prince William succeeded as Landgrave of Hesse, which made him the paramount ruler, and Rothschild became his banker. From a relationship that began with coin collecting came the basis for the fortune of the House of Rothschild.

In the beginning, since *numismatics,* or the collection of coins, was a man's hobby, it achieved several male faculties, one of which was a preoccupation with the detail and history of the coins, rather than any concern for their innate beauty. The word "numismatics" originates in the Greek *nomos,* meaning "law." Hence, *nomisma* means "anything sanctioned by law" or "legal tender." Eventually numismatics was to embrace much more than just coins, including the collection of medals and tokens and currency. The latter was a late refinement, for paper money has no inherent value, its monetary value being given by government. Its collection value is the proof of success of the hobby, since the value of paper money is much more a matter of faith and confidence than that of precious-metal coins or medals.

All these changes and the debasement, as of the Roman coinage system, created a harvest for European coin collectors, one that was not totally appreciated in the United States for a long time. A very respectable collection of ancient coins of many different varieties could be amassed in the middle of the twentieth century with very little capital investment. A follis of Constantine the Great could be purchased for a dollar, and those of Maxentius, Severus, and Galerius could be bought for $2 each. An antoninianus of Diocletian could be bought for $1.50, so could one of Probus and Maximianus. Many other antoniniani and folles could be bought for slightly more money. Even many denarii were not particularly costly. An Alexander Severus was valued at $2, Heliogabalus at $2.50, a Commodus also at $2.50, and scores of others were in this price range. Many, many other Roman coins of the Empire could be purchased for $10, $15, or $20 each.

Coins, Collectors and Counterfeiters

There were more valuable, more expensive coins, of course. The gold *aureus* of Tiberius might sell for $75. An aureus of Claudius was worth $120, one of Caligula was worth $150. Nor were the coins of the Roman Republic so very expensive that an average collector could not achieve a respectable group of them. The old as might sell for $25 each. Various denarii of the Republic, showing heads of Apollo and other gods and goddesses, might go for anything from $5 to $20. The various coins of the civil wars of Rome, which continued from 59 to 31 B.C., tend to be more valuable, because they were issued during a limited period. In the 1970's a Pompey denarius might sell for $17.50 and a Julius Caesar for $22.50. One factor that helped keep prices down was that in archaeological excavations, and even in plain gardening, people in Europe in the 1970's continued to unearth hoards of ancient coins. Some of these might be extremely valuable, as would be, for example, a hoard of the coins of Romulus Augustulus, who reigned from 475 and 476, or of Olybrius of 472, or of Sebastianus, 411. A gold aureus of Pompey the Great might bring as much as $500 at a sale. And in the 1970's, as more and more coin collectors joined the ranks, it was apparent that prices would go upward, not downward. Eventually, even the most common of ancient coins would leap ahead in value, for coin collecting as a general hobby was really quite young. In the 1930's the American who collected ancient coins was a rare bird, and he was warned by the numismatic writers to take extreme care in buying because the number of counterfeits was large, and the number of knowledgeable American dealers was small. The number of counterfeits certainly did not decrease in the years that passed, but by the 1970's the number of dealers in ancient coins had increased remarkably, and it was quite possible for anyone anywhere in the world to achieve a respectable collection of these fascinating coins.

7
Coin Collecting in the United States

What started coin collecting in America in a big way was the Indian head penny and the subsequent Lincoln head penny, which was first issued in 1909. As noted, some of those pennies turned out to be quite hard to find and became valuable. The 1914 Denver-mint penny in uncirculated condition, for example, was valued at $450 half a century later, and five years after minting, a 1960 penny with a small date was valued at $3.50. The 1877 Indian head penny could be worth $1,000.

Even in 1850, when millions of American coins had been struck, there were only about three hundred coin *collectors* in the United States. Fifty years later there were about a hundred thousand collectors. By the 1970's there were over ten million Americans who were interested in coins and amassing private collections. True numismatists, those who collect for the love of information and coins, often regard many of the millions of newcomers as fly-by-night speculators. In any event, coin collecting had become an important American hobby in a very short time, and in the 1970's an entire new industry, of publications and services for coin collectors, was thriving.

There were some two thousand coin clubs in existence in the United States, with the most active collectors—members of the American Numismatic Association—at the top of the heap, attempting to maintain some order in coin collecting and to prevent it from becoming too heavily speculative in nature.

Some of the most valuable coins of the twentieth century are the proof sets. These are specially made coins, struck from polished dies on polished metal blanks. In the beginning, proofs had a legitimate coining function. They were proofs made to test the coins. Later, special sets of proofs were made to honor various individuals—kings and visitors and political leaders. Finally, when coin collecting became a big business, proofs became a big business, too. The sale of proof coins to collectors and accumulators of coins was much like the sale of special philatelic sets and sheets of stamps to stamp collectors. The hobby in the twentieth century had quite outgrown those who simply wished to have representative coins of all nations.

Many factors combine to create or increase the value of coins. The most important, of course, is the dating of coins, because once the twelve-month period is past, no coin is again of the series of 1977 or whatever the year might be. Once an entire denomination goes out of circulation—like the United States half cent—the coins that remain are sure to rise in value, even though millions of them have been used. This has happened to the 20-cent piece that was minted between 1875 and 1878, the 3-cent silver piece, and the half-dime.

The 3-cent piece, for example, was minted from 1851 to 1873, the smallest coin ever struck by the United States Mint. It came into use because the price of silver rose along with wild rumors that accompanied the California gold strike of the 1840's, and suddenly the American silver dollars were worth $1.03 in terms of gold. Silver dollars then became in short supply, since they were hoarded, and the mint brought out this 3-cent coin to bring the dollar back.

The half-dime was odd in that the minters did not think it necessary to put any value on the coin. There were also some errors in minting, such as the break in the dies that resulted in a coin that said "1796 LIKERTY" and another that read "1800 LIBETKY."

Everyone in America is familiar with the American dime, but not many people other than coin collectors know that the proper spelling is *disme* (an old term for "one tenth"). The 20-cent piece, which was the result of somebody's idea that it would be effective to have a coin between dime and quarter, did not work out at all. The trouble was that whoever designed the 20-cent piece made it too close in size to the quarter. The quarter boasted milled edges, whereas the 20-cent piece's edges were smooth, but this was too subtle a difference. One of these coins, the issue called 1876 CC, is one of the rare finds in the history of American coin collecting. Only fourteen are known to exist. A proof copy has sold for $12,750.

Some ten thousand of these coins were minted without the letters *CC*.

Half dollars have been coined ever since 1794, and some of these proved to be quite odd—especially the one brought out in 1807 stamped with the value "20 cents." Dollars always created a problem as long as new supplies of silver were being discovered in the country, and the price of this mineral fluctuated. Consider the American dollar of 1804, which has turned out to be one of the more valuable coins of the world, in what is called Type I. (Type II, which is less valuable, is what is called a re-strike, or a reissue from the same dies.) The silver dollar of 1804 exists, as far as the coin world knows, in only half a dozen specimens, although the records of the mint show that nearly twenty thousand such dollars were struck that year. Why did they disappear? Well, it is known that in 1804 the silver dollar had more than a dollar's worth of silver in it—and so it was simple enough for merchants and others to buy the silver dollars and melt them down for the silver content.

One of the most interesting of American coins is the 5-cent piece, or nickel, which has been made since 1866 in four types—bearing a shield, a Liberty head, a buffalo or Indian head (depending on the side), and a likeness of Thomas Jefferson.

Not very many ardent coin collectors are likely to find shield-type nickels in circulation, but occasionally one comes out of some old cigar box or private hoard. The most valuable of them is the nickel of the year 1877, of which relatively few were made. It sold for around $800 in the middle of the twentieth century. Other good shield nickels were those of 1866, 1871, 1875, and 1877, all of which brought prices of $20 or more.

In 1883 the mint stopped making the shield nickels and began coining the Liberty head type, which were quite common in circulation in the 1920's and were often seen in the 1930's and 1940's. The designer of this nickel made a horrible error—he did not put the word "cents" on the coin. On the front was a likeness of Liberty. On the back was a Roman V encircled by an open wreath. So, many bright fellows gilded the new nickels with gold plate and passed them off as five-dollar gold pieces. The mint eventually retaliated by finding room for the inscription "cents."

The year 1912 was supposedly the last year that the Liberty head nickel was coined, but this is not entirely true. Mint employees have always been subjected to serious temptations, because most of them know a great deal about the value of coins. In the middle of the nineteenth century, when coin collecting began to attract a following, among the first to become aware of it were the employees of the Philadelphia mint. One old collector remembered how, in the beginning, he could always go down to the mint and buy new coins. He did so around the end of the year, knowing that the coins would be re-done with changed dates in the next year, and bought up the older ones, in mint condition, for trading purposes. Then, after a few seasons, he soon saw the change come over the mint people. *They* were taking the coins and putting them away for a rainy day, and substituting the new.

There was nothing illegal about that, but there was something illegal about what some mint employees did to the Liberty nickel. Learning that the nickel was to be replaced in 1913, several employees made up a special 1913 die and struck a number of coins. Half a dozen of these were sold to a dealer, and found their way into the collection of the famous Colonel E. H. R. Green, Wall Street millionaire and son of old Hetty Green. Colonel Green had begun as a stamp collector, then doubled his interests and turned to coin collecting as well. He bought the 1913 Liberty nickels and kept them in his collection for a number of years. Then, when his collection was broken up, these half dozen 1913 coins were sent flying to the winds—and in the middle of the century they were valued at around $10,000 each, although they were not, strictly speaking, anything more or less than forgeries.

Of the buffalo or Indian head nickels, the last of which were issued in 1937, at least one of the type, in mint condition, was valued at $4,000 by the middle of the twentieth century, and many in fine condition were valued at more than $10 apiece. Even several Jefferson nickels of the years 1938 to 1942 were valued at more than a dollar in used condition. It was not much wonder, then, that small boys in the 1960's and 1970's began rushing down to the dime store and picking up blue coin folders in order to start coin collections of their own.

8
Big Money in Coins

It is a sorry thing to say, but probably avarice is the leading factor in the remarkable growth of coin collecting in the past quarter of a century. But before anyone in America condemns coin collectors, let them at least examine the temptations. They are at least as great—and in many ways much greater than—the temptations besetting those who collect stamps or early American glass or French Impressionist paintings, or anything else that has a marketable value.

Until 1963 American coins were the most valuable in the world. The world's record price paid for a single coin had been the $29,000 given for an 1804 United States silver dollar, when one of the original dollars was sold in Los Angeles in 1961. This coin, known as the Idler-Hydeman specimen, then brought that high price, and some coin dealers thought the millennium had come.

Big Money in Coins

Then, in April, 1963, at Lake Lucerne in Switzerland a large gold piece coined in 303 by the Roman Emperor Maximianus I Herculius went under the gavel at an auction and brought $38,600. It was a large and unique piece, worth 10 aurei or 250 denarii. But what made it so valuable is that it was unique. It is the only gold piece of its kind known in the world today. The only other 10-aurei piece in the world, of a different type, is in a French museum. It was found in 1922.

A month later it became apparent that a new era had dawned for coin collectors, because another of the 1804 dollars was sold, and this one brought a new record price for American coins, $36,000. Since that time inflation and the increasing number of collectors has sent prices skyrocketing again and again. Consequently no book could conceivably reflect the unreal market values of coins. As the eminent numismatist Charles F. French put it, prices change almost every week in the coin markets. Values rise and keep rising so that collectors must refer to magazines and newspapers to keep themselves informed. But generally prices and values go up and up.

Why such prices? Because of the scarcity of such coins as the 1804 dollar and the Roman Emperor's special money. With the growth of coin collecting and the prosperity of the Western world seemingly growing year after year, those prices would soon be left far behind, and one day they would be doubled. Why not? What is the value of a unique piece of money or a unique work of art? It is whatever anyone wants to put on it.

Take the famous Liberty head nickels of Colonel Green's collection. At an auction in 1961 a bid of more than $40,000 was made for one of these pieces, but the owner had set a reserve bid of $50,000, below which he would not sell, and when no one would go that high, the coin remained unsold.

In the 1970's individual coin prices changed so rapidly that figures did not mean very much—except to show how valuable coins had become. And over the years there were many success stories. One from England recalls how the English had begun collecting American coins long before the Americans had done so. In 1964, in London, Lord St. Oswald of Wakefield, Yorkshire, authorized Christie's auction house to sell an old coin collection that had been in his family for many, many years. In the collection were pieces from the Cromwell Protectorate, coins from the days of Queen Anne, and other valuable and important British coins. All of these pieces had been carefully tagged and cataloged separately. Lord St. Oswald realized that he had a fortune in fabulous coins.

In one box, however, were a number of odds and ends that had been picked up by one of his lordship's forefathers during a trip to America in 1795. His lordship had seen the coins, and had not known much about them, so he had tossed them into a box. Included were some twenty 1794 uncirculated large cents, two uncirculated 1794 silver dollars, and many other uncirculated American coins of that period. His lordship's ancestor had either been one of that odd coterie of coin enthusiasts of the late eighteenth century in England, or he had carried a great pocketful of change around with him.

The value of these pieces was noted immediately by the cataloger, Albert Baldwin, but even he did not know the prices this odd lot would fetch at the sale. When the day came and the collection was sold, each of the 1794 dollars brought more than $11,000, and one of the 1794 pennies sold for $8,400. Altogether, the thirty-three lots of the odd box the gentleman had brought in so carelessly brought $72,000, or more than all the rest of his lordship's valuable collection.

Another extremely valuable coin is the 1822 half eagle, or $5 gold piece. In 1976 it was reported that only three of these coins remained in existence, although around eighteen thousand had been minted. Most books on coins simply called it very rare and did not give a value. One of these coins was in the United States Mint collection. Another had never been sold at public auction. The third one, which had been sold a few times, had been last valued at $20,000. But earlier it had been valued much higher by one man—J. Pierpont Morgan, the banker and collector.

This particular coin was purchased by coin collector William Forrester Dunham of Chicago from the estate of Harlan P. Smith in 1907. Two years later, when Pierpont Morgan was at the height of his collecting activity and was buying paintings, statuary, books, manuscripts, and other valuables, Morgan learned of the existence of this coin. He was ever the seeker of the unique, and since there were but three of the 1822 half eagles in the world, and since two of them were unavailable, this coin was as nearly unique as many other treasures he had acquired. He knew what many others did not—that value was directly connected with scarcity—and so Pierpont Morgan had not the slightest hesitation in offering $35,000 for the

half eagle. It was the highest price then ever offered anywhere for a single coin.

One type of silver dollar, the 1852 seated Liberty, was
valued at $2,500, another, the 1870 minted in San Fran-
cisco, was valued at $2,700. Another valuable dollar was
one that was never circulated in the United States as
money. This was the *trade dollar,* which was issued from
1873 to 1879. After that, only proofs were issued, not
dollars for circulation, and there were put out until 1885.
The last of those proofs was valued at $9,000.

The trade dollar was more valuable than the American
dollar—that is to say, it contained more silver. There was
a good reason for this—it was designed to use silver and
thereby to make the silver miners happy, and to stand on
its own feet in the Orient trade. It was developed to try
to compete with the Mexican government, which had been
as successful in introducing Mexican pesos into the China
trade, as the Austrians had been in bringing the Maria
Theresa thaler into the Middle East and Africa. The at-
tempt was not very successful, and regular coinage was
ended in 1879. Then someone in the mint either struck
proofs without authority or forgot to keep records. Apparently ten such proofs were struck in 1884 without
Congressional or Treasury authority; five more in 1885.
Nobody in the outside world seemed to know much about
this until 1908, when one of the dollars came up for sale.
Then the story was revealed. In the 1960's the 1884 proof
was later valued at $2,000, but by the 1970's it was said
to be worth $8,750.

There was very little supply but much demand for a
gold dollar before the discovery of gold at Sutter's Creek,

California. The American gold supply in the early years was found in North Carolina and Georgia, and some coins were minted in Charlotte and at Dahlonega, Georgia. One of the most valuable of these early coins was an 1849 dollar minted at Charlotte. One of these (apparently the only one in existence) sold for $6,000 in 1956.

Since the United States went off the gold standard during the first Franklin Roosevelt administration, few young Americans have ever seen gold pieces outside museums (though gold coins have again been generally available since 1976). Gold coins have jumped in value much more than silver coins because of the scarcity of the metal. The $2.50 gold piece is about the size of a dime. It was called a quarter eagle, because the $10 gold piece was the standard gold coin, and all other gold pieces derive their names from the eagle, or $10 piece. The first of these quarter eagles was issued in 1796, the last in 1929. The least valuable of them is worth $25 and the most valuable is worth $10,000—this is the proof of the 1841 coin minted at Philadelphia, and nobody knows how many of them were made. Often it is just listed and not valued at all. Several quarter eagles have been sold at prices of $5,000 and more.

At about the same time that someone had the bright idea of coining a 3-cent piece of silver—which was to be used to buy stamps, since the first-class postage of the country was then fixed at 3 cents per letter—someone, perhaps the same person, had the idea that it would also be useful to coin a three-dollar gold piece for those who wanted to buy lots of stamps. So it was done in 1854, after a long Congressional debate in 1853, in which the debaters made it quite clear that they wished to help the metal miners of California and other regions. The gold piece was issued until 1889, and then the postal rates were changed, so there was no conceivable excuse for continuing to put it out.

The $3 gold piece was never very popular. This is a boon to $3-gold-piece owners of the 1970's, because the coins are most valuable. The cheapest, which was the issue of 1854—the very first—was valued at $145. The most expensive, potentially, was the piece struck in San Francisco in 1870, of which only two are known to exist. Its value can be shown by comparing the price for which one of the proofs of the piece of 1875 sold—and there were ten times as many of those. A century after minting the 1875 piece was valued at around $10,000.

The next denomination of gold pieces is most valuable of all in comparison to its intrinsic worth because only 450 of them were made over four years, and they were never placed in circulation. This is the $4 piece, or *stella* (so called after the large star on the back). In the 1970's those coins were valued at between $6,000 and $13,000.

One of the first American coins issued by the federal government was the $5 gold piece, or half eagle, and such coins were issued until 1929, but oddly, until 1807 there was no indication on the coin as to its value, which was confusing, to say the least. The outstanding rarity among these is the piece of 1822, which was valued at around $20,000, and it is assumed from the very small number of these coins in existence that most of them were melted down that year.

The eagle, the standard gold coin, did not carry a value

until 1838. Oddly enough, not one of them comes anywhere near the value of the scarce 1822 half eagle. The
most valuable eagle is the issue of 1798 with six stars
and the issue of 1858 from Philadelphia. These are worth
about a quarter of the price of the half eagle of 1822.

The double eagle, or $20 gold piece, was the most valu-
able piece of coined money ever issued in the United
States by the government, and it came out only after gold
was discovered in California. In that first year was issued
what is probably the most valued of all American coins,
although it is doubtful if a price will ever be placed on it.
One—and only one—double eagle of 1849 was made by
the mint, and that was placed in the collection of the
United States Treasury. It was a prize to whet the appetite
of even old J. Pierpont Morgan.

Among the more valuable of American coins and the
oddities of the coin world are a number of private coins
issued by individuals over the years. During the 1830's a
man named Templeton Reid issued $200,000 worth of
gold coins. It was later discovered that the gold in them
was worth more than the face value of the coins, and so
most of them were melted down. These coins are extremely rare and valuable, rated in the past at prices between $600 and $4,000 each. Mostly they were called
very rare in the 1970's. Other coins, issued by the Bechtler
family in North Carolina, have become valuable for the
same reason, and some of their $5 gold pieces are valued
at $1,500 and more.

The most interesting gold coins in America were made
in various ways in and near the mining fields of California.
The Moffat company of California put out a gold ingot

said to be worth $14.25. A century afterward it was worth around $10,000. Oregon, the Beaver State, issued its own coins in 1849, bearing the likeness of a beaver. The $10 gold piece was worth $10,000 in 1976.

Coin collectors—the big collectors who invest large amounts of money—run the danger of standing some large losses as well as profits. In the 1960's, when the supply of silver money became short—partly because of the demands of coin collectors and partly because of a shortage of silver—a store of silver dollars was thrown onto the money market by the Treasury. Silver dollars had long been a drag on the market, used largely in the Western states, where they were symbols of the good old days, were often put into dollar slot machines, and were used on the gaming tables of Nevada. Among the other silver dollars thrown out so suddenly were a quantity of the 1903 dollar minted in New Orleans (a mint that closed down in 1904). Well, that quantity of dollars put a serious crimp in some pocketbooks. The 1903 New Orleans dollar had been worth $1,500 before the market was flooded, but in a month and a half the price had dropped to $15. Later it rose again, but in the 1970's it was still worth only $40.

Early in the 1970's the federal government's General Services Administration decided to please coin enthusiasts and make some money for the Treasury at the same time. GSA offered to sell $3 million in silver dollars minted at Carson City, Nevada, between 1870 and 1890. Two million of these were sold to dealers and the public at prices up to $30 each. Some dealers acquired large hoards of these dollars and held them to create a scarcity.

The government, with its stock of a million dollars, still did not know what to do with them in 1976. A wrong move—dumping dollars on the market—could stampede collectors.

Not all the big money or big value in coins is to be found in American coins by far, as might be suspected by the discovery of the valued Roman ten-aurei pieces. In a 1963 auction, a record was broken by a Canadian dollar of 1911 (only four are known to exist), which sold for $50,000. Some Canadian pennies are worth between $150 and $200, and one, called the 1936 dot because of an imperfection, was worth about $4,000 in the 1970's. A King George V five-cent piece was valued in 1966 at $2,500, and the number of Canadian dimes worth $1,000 or more was considerable. A 1921 King George V fifty-cent piece was valued at $6,000.

One of the world's great coins is a five-franc piece showing a likeness of Prince Louis Napoleon, issued in 1851. In 1875 that coin was offered for sale at an auction in Paris (the Europeans were dealing hotly in coins while American collectors were still in swaddling clothes). This particular coin was run up in price to 113 francs before it was sold, and the American coin fancier George Mathews, who happened to be at the auction, asked the unsuccessful bidder why he had gone so high as 110 francs (about $27.50). It was a piece with the lock of hair, he was told. The puzzled American investigated and discovered that after the coup d'etat that overthrew the Second Republic in 1851, the Prince-President had decreed that his likeness should go on the coins of France. The proposed new five-franc piece was brought to his attention, but he laid it aside for a few days in the press of other business. The director of the mint, hearing nothing to the contrary, went ahead with the coining. Then, one day the Prince-President discovered the likeness, and objected to a lock of hair that curled over near the temple. He ordered it taken off the coin. But twenty-three coins had been issued with the lock in place before it could be chiseled off the die, and so this became a great coin collector's rarity.

Another rarity of quite a different type was discovered in Hawaii in 1931 by a marine named Raymond C. Waits. One day on the beach between Barbers Point and Nankuli, he discovered a tarnished piece of copper. He took it home and polished it up, to reveal a coin, a penny from England of the time of William III. It was dated "Britannia, 1699."

That penny found its way into the Bishop Museum. No one ever answered the question, How did a British penny of 1699 find its way to the west end of Oahu Island? From the ship of Captain James Cook, in the middle of the eighteenth century?

There are valuable coins of all nations, particularly those nations that have issued gold or silver coins. The 1893 R. Guanajuato Mexican five-peso gold piece is exceedingly rare, and so it is very valuable. Records show that only sixteen were minted. Someday it will be worth a fortune. The 1888 G. Hermosillo five-peso piece does not even have mint records, it is so rare, and the 1888 Ro Potosí ten-peso piece is so rare that only one is known to exist.

9
Commemorative Coins

Whenever some ruler wished to be sure that he went down in history, he was likely to issue a commemorative coin, on the principle that the intrinsic value of the coin would keep people from destroying it. Julius Caesar and other Roman rulers commemorated their military victories thus, and the practice spread throughout the world and the ages.

The United States began issuing commemorative coins in 1892 in order to raise money for the World's Columbian Exposition at Chicago. The coins were issued at a face value of 50 cents, but they were sold for a dollar. That established the principle in the United States, and thereafter all commemorative coins were sold for twice their face value or more. In about seventy-five years the United States then issued some 157 kinds of commemorative coins —quarter eagles, half dollars (forty-eight of those), dollars of gold and silver, and $50 gold pieces.

Some of those commemorative pieces became quite valuable. The Columbian Exposition pieces did not—they could be purchased in the 1970's for $10 or less. Yet a 1922 Grant Memorial half dollar with star would bring $150, a 1928 Hawaii sesquicentennial half dollar cost $500, and a 1915 Panama-Pacific Exposition $50 gold piece was worth $5,000.

That Columbian half dollar was not much of a succcess any way you wanted to look at it. It was minted on November 19, 1892, and it was intended that the coin should be sold at the opening of the fair. But then the fair got bogged down in construction, and one thing led to another, and in the end, although 28 million people went to the World's Columbian Exposition in Chicago in 1893, only 2 million of the 5 million half dollars were sold. So, at the end of the fair, with this big surplus, some of them were put into general circulation as half dollars and became part of the United States coinage. This was a matter of some annoyance to the manager of the fair, and to the people who had bought the 2 million coins at twice their face value. Eventually, a million and a half of these half dollars were melted down for new coinage. The most impressive part of that Columbian Exposition was not the coinage, by far, but the Egyptian Village, which contained Oriental dancers, including a belly dancer called Little Egypt. This was the high point of the exposition, and that fact was recalled even fifty years later in a book that described the coinages of the Columbian Exposition of 1893.

In 1899, when American schoolchildren contributed some $50,000 to the erection of a statue of General Lafayette in Paris, the United States government decided to strike a commemorative coin to honor the French general who had done so much to help secure American freedom. So the Lafayette dollar was coined. Fifty thousand were made, and 14,000 of these were melted down later, so 36,000 were put into circulation at $2 each. Under United States law, coins were always to be minted in the year stamped on their faces or backs (that law was honored as much in the breach as in the practice, over the years). This coin was actually minted in 1899 although it said "1900" on the face. (That was because the Paris exposition was being held in 1900 and that was the point of the statue.) The first of these coins that was minted was sent to President McKinley, and he sent it on to President Loubet of France.

McKinley's name figured in another commemorative American coin, the gold dollar of the Louisiana Purchase Exposition, which was held in St. Louis in 1904.

President McKinley had authorized this exposition, and it was indicated that a special gold dollar would be coined to commemorate it and help raise money to finance the fair. This dollar was to depict Thomas Jefferson, who was President during the period when the Louisiana Territory was bought from Napoleon. It was to sell not for twice, but for three times its face value. Some twenty million visitors came to the fair, but only 17,500 of these dollars were sold. Sometime after McKinley's assassination, and before the coins went on sale, it was decided to issue a special gold dollar with the McKinley figure on it, to be a commemorative of that President, too, in a way. But, as at the Columbian Exposition, there was a lack of communication between the coiners and the fair managers and the public, and the coins did not do at all well. In an effort to stimulate sales, the managers fixed up special mountings in the form of gold stickpins, bangles, charms, and bracelets, and a dollar was put into the bowl of a souvenir spoon. Still, the sale of souvenir coins failed, and at the end of the fair 215,000 of them were melted down, and the gold was returned to the Treasury. Sixty years later both the Jefferson and McKinley gold dollar were valued at $100.

The Lewis and Clark Centennial Exposition in 1904, 1905, and 1906 was the occasion for another special coinage. A maximum of 250,000 gold dollars were authorized, and 65,000 were actually coined. But in the end 40,000 were melted down, and so the coins, again, increased in value, until half a century later they were worth more than $400 each.

When the Panama Canal was completed to link the Atlantic and Pacific shipping lanes, the United States government celebrated with another international exposition, the Panama-Pacific Exposition, which was held in two parts, in San Diego in 1914 and in San Francisco in 1915. For this exposition the government authorized the coining of the only $50 gold pieces ever made officially in the United States, and thus created a valuable rarity for numismatists. The reason for allowing $50 pieces was the recognition of the special place of California in the history of gold, and remembrance that in the days of the mining furor, the Californians had used $50 pieces that were locally made.

The $50 coins were made in two varieties, one round, and one octagonal. Both bore the same inscription and the head of Minerva on one side and an owl on the other. A fourteen-ton hydraulic press was shipped to San Francisco from the Philadelphia mint for the sole purpose of striking these coins. In the beginning it went very well, and on June 15, 1915, at a public ceremony the first one hundred gold pieces were struck. Then three of the dies broke in the plate of the round pieces, and everything was stopped while they were being repaired.

The Panama-Pacific Exposition was a heyday for the growing number of coin collectors in America. Farran Zerbe, a very-well-known numismatist, was head of the Coin and Medal Department, and he displayed some twenty thousand coins at the exposition. (Later his collection became part of the world-famous collection of the Chase Manhattan Bank of New York.) Two other coins were made for the exposition, a gold dollar and a gold quarter eagle ($2.50). Twenty-five thousand of the dollars were used and 6,700 of the quarter eagles, and 483 round and 645 octagonal $50 pieces were sold. These became the most valued of all American commemorative coins. In the 1960's the round coins sold at $5,000 and the octagonal coins at $4,500.

Dozens of other American events were celebrated by the striking of special coins sold at special ceremonies or expositions. A half dollar was struck to memorialize the centennial of the Monroe Doctrine in 1923, another in 1925 for the California Diamond Jubilee, and one in 1926 to commemorate the pioneers who followed the Oregon trail. Occasionally the coins were gold dollars or gold quarter eagles, but the last of these was struck in 1926 to commemorate the Philadelphia Sesquicentennial.

Thereafter the coinage was confined to half dollars, these being more within the reach of the majority of collectors, and the silver supply being used in preference to the gold.

In the twentieth century the influence of coin collectors has definitely been felt in American coinage. It showed itself in many ways. The United States government issued some sixty commemoratives altogether, most of them in the twentieth century, and most of them in silver. But there were more than two hundred different varieties, and the creation of varieties was more an idea of collectors than it was respresentative of a need for employment at the mints.

Governments in recent years have discovered a new source of revenue in coin collectors. In the United States in 1936, the government began selling specially struck proof coins, made with polished dies struck against polished blanks, creating superior coins not intended for circulation as money. These coins were made from 1936 to 1942, then during World War II coinage of proofs was stopped as an unnecessary expense and activity. It was resumed in 1950. The coins struck are the cent, nickel, dime, quarter, and half dollar. Altogether this came to a monetary value of 91 cents, but the coins are sold at $2.10 to collectors, which creates income for the government.

The sale of proof sets became a very big business in the 1960's. In 1964, after the assassination of President John F. Kennedy, sales of proof sets of American coins reached nearly four million sets. That included an Eisenhower silver dollar, a Kennedy half dollar, a Washington quarter, a Roosevelt dime, a Jefferson nickel, and a Lincoln penny. Collectors and dealers believed they had reached an all-time high, prompted by the interest in the new "memorial" Kennedy half dollar.

But in 1976, America's bicentennial year, the sale of proof sets went past the four-million mark. There simply were no unbreakable records in this growing hobby.

Other countries have certainly understood the revenue value of coins for collectors. In 1966, for example, when the Bahama Islands decided to change from the British system based on pounds, shillings, and pence to the decimal system of coinage, it offered to collectors, months before the changeover, two packages of the new coins. There were to be nine coins in all, ranging from the $5 down to the 1 cent. The complete set, valued at considerably less than the $9.06 U.S. that the coins added up to in dollars, sold for $16.00 U.S. The small set, including all but the expensive $5 and $2 pieces, sold for $5.25 U.S. These sets made a neat profit for the Bahaman government. They were sold by the Bahamas Ministry of Finance.

Some nations, such as Israel, discovered that it was profitable to establish special corporations to deal with numismatists. Israel pioneered the establishment of its Government Coins and Medals Corporation, and a whole new field of finance opened to the government. Coins in special sets, medals, and special coin-medals could be and were struck by the dozens for the sale to collectors. One complete series of special coin-medals was struck to celebrate the historic cities of Israel, with nine cities so honored. A bronze coin-medal honoring Jerusalem, for example, was valued at $4 and a silver one was sold for $14. Other cities were Ashkelon, Acre, Tiberias, Beit-

She'an, Avdat, Caesarea, Jaffa, and Lod. Not only were special sets sold, but special carrying cases and special albums were designed to hold and display these coins and medals.

There were many ways of calling attention to coins and creating values in them. When Britain issued a special commemorative crown to honor the late Winston Churchill, one American firm offered three different varieties of holders for the crown. Some were printed in color, showing the Churchill coat of arms and the British coat of arms, famous quotations by and about Churchill, and were encased in vinyl. Others, less expensive, boasted only some of these extras.

Canada also learned about special sets and commemorative coins. In 1966 it began plans for its Centennial Celebration, and of course this included a whole schedule of activity on the coin front. A special $20 gold coin and six other coins were planned for a set to be sold by the government, and these would be placed in plush-lined leatherette cases and sold at about $40. The government cheerfully hoped to sell a hundred thousand or more of such sets to collectors, at a profit to the mint.

By the middle of the twentieth century, then, government had become deeply involved in the business of coin collection. It was probable that, as time passed, ever more types and varieties of coins would be offered to the bewildered world.

Coin collecting had reached one apex—but that was not to say that it would not start a new orbit and reach another. In the spring of 1966, the United States Mint had to cut off its supply of special mint sets of American coins because the demand was so great for the 1965 sets. This, even though the United States, like most governments, had long since been limiting purchases to ten sets per customer in order to discourage dealers from trying to monopolize the new issues of coins. At the same moment, the supply of American silver dollars was almost wiped out—none had been coined for years, but until the 1960's there had been no shortage. When collectors began prizing them and the United States debased its silver coinage, then the old heavy silver dollars quite disappeared, and all that were left were those controlled in the mints and siphoned out carefully until the big GSA sale of 1973 and 1974. With the international shortage in the supply of silver, coin collectors in the 1970's were very definitely a threat to the well-being of various national currencies, too.

Or, if "threat" seems too strong to describe a group that contributed to various treasuries so handsomely, "necessary nuisance" might be a better term.

Proofs and special sets became objects of speculation and investment by various collectors and accumulators of coins. For example, in 1931 in Britain the government issued five sets of what was called Maundy Money (from an ancient practice of the kings of passing out money to the poor). These five sets, in red and white leather bags, consisted of twenty-six silver coins, which added up to King George V's age at that time, sixty-six years. In 1964 each set was worth $250 in New York.

That same year a 1944 set of South Africa proof coins, eight in all, with a total value of not more than two American dollars, was selling for $150. It was not even twenty years old.

Coins, Collectors and Counterfeiters

Here are some of the other proof offerings of various governments, sold to make profit for the treasuries and to satisfy the urges of coin addicts. In 1937 the British put out a coronation medal to honor George VI (as they did with Queen Elizabeth II and had with all monarchs before). In 1940, as every year, the Vatican issued a special series of coins and medals, honoring the Pope of the day. In the 1950's New Zealand, South Africa, Ghana, Ceylon —and nearly every government—issued special coins and medals not intended for circulation as money, but for the collections of private individuals who were willing to pay' handsomely for the objects.

10
Paper Currency
of the World

Paper money originated in China during the Ming dynasty, around 1400. The first paper money was printed on mulberry bark, which is very thin and very tough. It was large in size, hard to handle, and it was carefully guarded by the order of the Emperor. Anyone who counterfeited this money was subject to instant punishment—death. The warning was printed right on the money itself.

The ancestor of paper money in the Western world, if not in the Eastern, was not really this Chinese money but the clay tablets used for money by the ancients of the Fertile Crescent. Paper money, of course, was only as good as the faith of the people in the power that issued the money. In China the Emperor issued the paper money and stood behind it. Elsewhere other governments or banks or merchant houses issued pieces of paper promising to pay in goods or in valuable metals. In the southern

American colonies, tobacco was used to back up the tobacco-notes currency on which the economy subsisted.

Paper money is very closely tied to banking, which is a function of a highly specialized society. Consequently the wide use of paper money did not begin until the seventeenth century in England, although it began slightly earlier in the American colonies, where coins were in short supply. In the nineteenth century, nearly everywhere, money was issued in paper form by banks and by governments, but it represented almost always a promise to pay in specie or hard money. It was only in the twentieth century that paper money was backed by the unsupported statement of governments and not by their proved promise to pay in coin.

Many coin collectors look down on those who collect paper currency as being untrue to the real spirit of numismatics, traitors in a sense. But there is as much interest in paper money, or almost as much, as there is in coins, and there are some very valuable pieces of paper currency that have no intrinsic value at all. They are not even backed by any government anymore. Their value, as with postage stamps, is simply that of scarcity—because there are a great number of people who are interested in these pieces of paper.

The interest in paper currency, like that in stamps, is not nearly so easy to understand as that in coins. After all, one can at least melt down a gold or silver coin and make a bauble out of it, or fill a hole in a tooth with it, but a piece of paper has no value except what others believe it has. And yet such pieces of paper as the Sveriges Riksbank issues of the late seventeenth century are valuable.

Those from 1661 to 1667 bring almost whatever any owner wants to ask. Most of these pieces are in museums, and some of the last sold on the market have brought between seven hundred and a thousand Swedish crowns. Not bad for a piece of paper.

Some of the most interesting paper money is the Continental currency of the American Revolution, which was issued in denominations that went down as low as 10 cents, and the Confederate money of the Civil War, which gives a good picture of the privations of the South. (Some of it was printed on wallpaper, when the Confederacy was in desperate straits for imports of banknote paper.)

Until World War II it was very easy to obtain a collection of Confederate paper currency in almost any store in the South that specialized in relics of the Civil War. Many storekeepers used Confederate notes as giveaways and advertising devices to bring trade into their stores. But since the end of World War II and the huge growth in the collection of money, all real Confederate currency has worth, and some of it has grown quite valuable in the last few years. Here are some valuable examples. Notes known as the first Richmond Interest notes, the $50 Commerce and Industry note, the $100 Railroad Train note are all valuable. The July 25, 1861, issue called the Manouvrier note for $5 and a $20 note of the September 2, 1861, issue showing navigation and a globe were highly valued by one dealer in the 1970's. Only a few years earlier one could have had them for fractions of the price—and some of them for nothing at all.

Some very high prices were being offered. In the middle of the twentieth century, for example, one New York dealer was offering as much as $500 for a rare $100 United States silver certificate, which seemed a high price—except that $240 for a rare $2 silver certificate represented much more of a profit on investment or speculation, or whatever one wishes to call it. There was no question about the values existing for the students and collectors of paper money. As with any other specialty, it was just a question of knowing one's way around, knowing *when* to buy and collect and *what* to buy and collect. Many experts existed the world around to advise the amateur, and even to tout him.

One interesting type of collection of United States money is that of fractional currency—money of less than a dollar in denomination. This money was issued during the Revolution and at various other times. It was especially common during the Civil War when hoarders drove the supply of silver and copper money out of the market. The first issue of this fractional money came in 1862 in the form of postage stamps, of all things, and these were declared to be legal tender in payment of debts of less than five dollars. This emergency issue was supplanted by notes printed in denominations of 5 cents, 10 cents, and 50 cents. In 1863 and 1864 more fractional currency was issued, and again in 1869, when money was still short. This time a 3-cent note was issued, which was so badly used by the public that it became quite rare. The last of the fractional currency was issued in 1876.

America's bicentennial celebration of 1976 marked the reissuance of a form of paper money whose ups and downs told a good deal about the people of the United States and their history. It was the $2 bill.

Paper Currency of the World

The first $2 note issued by the United States government appeared in 1862, and for many years the bill was useful and popular. With the coming of horse and dog racing, $2 bills became a symbol of the track. Some people believed they were unlucky and would cut off the corners to remove "the curse." In the 1950's and 1960's the bill became very unpopular, and in 1966 the Treasury suspended production and took the $2 bills out of circulation.

But the inflation of the 1970's created a huge demand for $1 bills. An average of 1.6 billion dollar bills were printed and circulated each year. The $2 bill was expected to cut the government's cost of making paper money, saving perhaps $7 million in printing costs each year.

Among foreign currencies that have been of great interest (although until recently of little value) were the handsome ruble notes of the Russian monarchy, which lost all their value when the revolutionaries seized the government and pulled Russia out of World War I. They have since acquired value as collector's items.

Another interesting form of paper money that was once quite easy and cheap to collect was the German *Notgeld*, paper money issued during the terrible inflation that struck Germany after her defeat in World War I. Just before World War II it was still possible to purchase a German billion-mark note of this period for $2 or $3. If it had been redeemable in real money, this note would have been worth $400 million at the then rate of exchange. Actually, it had been reduced to nothing but a collector's item by the devaluation and changes in the German currency.

Students of currency, as well as students of coins, claim

that they learn a great deal about the world in their collecting, and there is certainly something in the claim. Who would believe that at one time a banknote was issued by the Chinese bank, honoring Marx and Lenin and bearing their pictures? And who would believe, even further, that this was done long before the Communists conquered China?

Well, it was. It was done in the fall of 1931, by the order of the First National Workers, Peasants, and Soldiers Representative Conference at Juichin, Kiangsi Province. It marked the establishment of the Central Democratic Workers and Peasants Government of China. The Communists ordered the production of silver and copper coins, and the Worker-Peasant Bank of China issued notes in the amount of a dollar, bearing the pictures of the German and Russian fathers of the Communist international revolution. The Communists were driven out of Kiangsi three years later and made their long march to Yenan in Shensi Province, where they lived in caves and survived until after World War II, when they arose in the ashes of the Japanese Empire and took command of a faltering China. But these notes were legal tender in Chinese Communist areas for a few months during the struggle of the 1930's.

In the twentieth century nearly all nations issued paper money, and some issued practically nothing else, or coins of so little intrinsic value (as those of aluminum compounds) that the paper money was preferable in the eyes of all.

Many states and possessions issued currency at one time or another, and then abandoned the practice for some reason. One example is Zanzibar, which became a British protectorate in 1890, and issued paper currency between 1908 and 1935. This money is highly prized by collectors because it is so rare—and it should be rare, for Zanzibar (which jointly with Tanganyika formed the United Republic of Tanzania in 1964) contains only about 300,000 people.

"Everyone interested in collecting money might consider collecting the currency of his native land, particularly the smaller denominations, because here he can have a relatively complete collection over a period of years without much outlay of expense." This is the point of view of one dealer in paper money.

In the middle of the 1970's, in the United States, there was in circulation nearly $170 for every person in the country. It was composed of a dozen denominations, six different types of money, and some eight hundred varieties. Here was enough to give a collector food for thought for many a moon, right down to the new two-dollar bill issued in the spring of 1976.

Of course, this includes the Federal Reserve notes, which run up to $10,000 in denomination, but there are not very many of those in circulation in any year, nor was it likely that there would be very many collectors for this.

For those who wished to collect something exotic, let them consider the chessbacks of Ströbeck. These pieces of paper money were made by the German town of Ströbeck, in those years at the end of World War I when metal was scarce. They might be called a part of the *Notgeld* of the period, the emergency money used when the government had failed to control its currency.

Coins, Collectors and Counterfeiters

The chessbacks celebrated the importance of chess in this little town. Chess was important because in the year 1011 the Count of Gungelin was imprisoned there in solitary confinement in a castle, and while there the count taught his jailers to play chess.

These pieces of paper money were issued to be used as currency and also to attract attention to the little town. For the collector of paper money it is fortunate that there are scores of stories much like that one, and thousands of ways of collecting paper currency, either spending a fortune or very little of what noncollectors call money. And for the beginning collector of the 1970's the acquisition of paper money from many places could sometimes be easier and cheaper than the beginning of any other kind of numismatic collection.

11
Counterfeit!

After many years of quiet, in the spring of 1966 the professional numismatists of the world announced hopefully that the problems of forgeries in coins and paper currency for collectors was not as serious as it had been a few months earlier. Why? Because for the first time the serious numismatists of the world were ready to talk openly about forgeries of coins and to help one another in tracing forgers and forgeries. There were many of both— scarcely any valuable coin does not have its forgeries. An expert metal engraver does not find it too hard to alter a coin (by changing an eight to a three or vice versa) or the unwary amateur collector may be fooled into buying a "gold piece" that is actually gilded copper.

Since the 1960's numismatics has improved constantly in the matter of cooperation, but as coins have become ever more valuable, the forgeries have also increased.

Forgeries exist all over Europe and in America. Forging

of coins has been popular in Japan for three hundred years, with special emphasis on the old-fashioned coins made before the modern day came to Japan in the middle of the nineteenth century. The Japanese once used holed coins such as those of China, and these were subject to much forgery. So were the kinds of money known as "bean money" and "bar money." Sometimes forgers simply pinched a piece off a metal pipe and made what looked very much like a coin of the period before 1870.

In 1804, after counterfeiters found it possible to reproduce those Spanish coins and the strikeover of George III, the Bank of England issued its famous Bank of England dollar. This piece showed the seal of Britannia on the back side and on the front side the King's head. Counterfeiters were quick to copy, making dollars that looked like the real thing but contained much less silver. Finally the British government made counterfeiting of silver and gold an offense punishable by death or by transportation to a far colony. Then the counterfeiters turned to copper coins, since counterfeiting these was only a misdemeanor. Further, they had something going for them. Most people in England—at least these who habitually used copper coins—could not read. The counterfeiters grew so bold that they made their own designs and then claimed that they were not counterfeit at all! This confusion was not ended until 1816, when the British government adopted steam-driven presses on which it made its coins, and invented a coin called the sovereign.

One of the most notorious counterfeiters of all time was François Lagrange of France, who began by forging postage stamps, Gauguin paintings, and Italian-school paintings. Finally Lagrange became an expert at forging

Counterfeit!

French, British, Dutch, American, and Swedish bank-notes. He might never have been caught, except—but that is part of the story.

Lagrange began his career as a forger of postage stamps. The year was 1927, and following World War I, Europe had begun to return to something like normal. At least collectors were collecting, and there was money to be made in the postage-stamp business. Lagrange came to the attention of a stamp dealer when he won a prize in a Swiss competition for the design of a new postage stamp. The dealer persuaded him to forge the valuable early postal issues of Mauritius and the early American postmaster stamp issues. He made what he said was one "superb" British Guiana stamp.

At this time Lagrange was in love with a girl of expensive tastes named Paulette, and he spent his money on her. Then he fell in love with another girl named Marilyn and gave up Paulette. Marilyn turned out to be even more expensive than Paulette, and Lagrange was constantly in need of money, so much that he looked for extra ways to make it, beyond the forging of stamps and an occasional French Impressionist painting.

One day he totted up his bills and learned that he owed half a million francs to various creditors.

That same day he was approached by an ugly little man who suggested that he join a counterfeiting ring as the chief engraver. The ugly man's name was Delanoit. He was the most feared man in the Parisian underworld. Delanoit asked Lagrange how much he received as his cut in forging stamps for the dealer. Twenty percent of the take, said Lagrange. So they arranged that Lagrange would receive 20 percent of the income from forging

British sterling notes and American $50 and $100 bills.

There was only one catch, said Delanoit, tapping the slighter Lagrange on the breastbone with a pudgy finger —he must not get big ideas and believe that he could pass the phoney money without the gang. The last engraver who had done that was now sitting on the bottom of the Seine in a tub of lard.

"I hope I will not offend my Anglo-Saxon friends," Lagrange wrote later. "I confess that I found the manufacture of both the pound sterling and the dollar to be mere child's play."

He obtained the proper materials, the papers, the inks, and the pens and brushes and steel. Within two weeks his first bills were in circulation and within a month he was a millionaire. But Marilyn, his lovely Marilyn, was still more expensive. When she learned that he could and would buy her what she wished, she wanted emeralds and ermines. Soon she had them. Soon, also, Lagrange was deeply in debt again. He could think of only one solution. He must forget Delanoit's warning and go into business for himself.

Lagrange was wise enough not to try to double-cross Delanoit. He told Delanoit that he wanted to begin the "private manufacture" of French government francs. Sheer stupidity, said Delanoit. The forging of foreign currency in Paris was a crime punishable by a small fine and, very seldom, imprisonment, but it was not then regarded as a major offense. The forgery of the currency of France was something else again—the authorities had no sense of humor about their own money.

Lagrange was too stubborn to listen to Delanoit's objections. He went ahead with his new venture. He was very successful. He organized his own counterfeit ring, the passers flooded France with counterfeit francs, and within a matter of months he had paid off all his debts.

Yet the very notes he forged bore the official warning: "Article 139 of the penal code punishes by forced labor those who counterfeit or falsify bank notes authorized by the law."

For many months Lagrange falsified the highest denominations. These notes were always changed in banks where money was given the closest scrutiny, and yet he was not suspected and his money "passed" every day of the year. Lagrange was on top of the world.

One day he ran into his old flame Paulette, and found her looking more beautiful than ever. He began seeing her again. A few days later, Paulette said that Marilyn knew about their relationship. Lagrange told her not to worry, he would take care of Marilyn. But he was wrong. One day at his door came a knock. When he answered, there were two inspectors of the Sûreté Nationale waiting for him. "Article one hundred thirty-nine of the Penal Code . . ." they said, and Lagrange knew. Marilyn had done him in.

The police went directly to his studio and tore down the bookcases that concealed his workroom, and the plates he used. They knew exactly where to look. Marilyn had told them everything she knew. So Lagrange, the greatest forger in France, was arrested.

While he was in prison, awaiting trial, Lagrange learned the story of another French counterfeiter who was every bit as skillful as he was. This was Fernand, who could make perfect bills. But Fernand chose to make only small bills, being a man of simple tastes, and not to make perfect bills. In the space on each bill in the little printed box where the warning about Article 139 appeared, Fernand always left a blank. Thus his bills were imperfect.

When Fernand was caught and arrested for violating Article 139, he denied that he had done any counterfeiting. He pointed to the empty space on the bill where the warning about Article 139 should have been. It was blank. He was not counterfeiting, he said, but simply making his own money. How could he be held responsible if people chose to take his money instead of the government's?

Fernand got off with a sentence of six months and that was suspended.

But Lagrange, poor Lagrange, was sentenced to the maximum punishment the law could devise—one considered by some to be worse than execution by guillotine. He was to be transported to Devil's Island in French Guiana. The convicts called Devil's Island the "dry guillotine." All this came because François Lagrange was too successful at his art. Among other improvisations, Lagrange had set up a real printing business and had sent off samples of paper from real American, French, British, and other notes to paper manufacturers. His orders were huge, and he read human nature correctly. The paper manufacturers in various countries had hired chemists to analyze these papers, and had been unwittingly in his service, forging French government and other government papers for him so that he could make his perfect notes. It was a wonderful scheme while it lasted, but Lagrange would spend the next quarter of a century remembering what Delanoit had told him.

12
...And More Counterfeit

As François Lagrange learned to his sorrow, governments are far more jealous than men and women when it comes to their right to make all the money of the country. In England, for example, in the seventeenth century it was high treason to counterfeit the government's coin. The offender was dragged to the gallows on a sledge. There he was hanged by the neck, but not until dead, because his entrails must be cut out and burned while he was still alive. Then his head was cut off, and his body was divided into four quarters, and hung in public places as a warning to all others.

It was enough to give a man something to think about. Yet in the sixteenth and seventeenth centuries, thousands of men counterfeited English currency. Counterfeiting was almost as common a crime in English society as stealing, and far more common than highway robbery, which was also punishable by death. Nearly everyone at least clipped coins. The general populace was never much in sympathy with the stern rulings of the governments regarding counterfeiters. That was because the general population did not understand the deathly fear of governments that counterfeiters would bring them to ruin.

Counterfeiting flourished so in England, in spite of the awful punishment, that in 1750 the Bank of England's authorities said that almost half the copper money circulating in that country was counterfeit.

For their crimes many counterfeiters were "transported" to the New World and set up in business after their sentences had been served. One of these was Joshua Dean, of London, who was convicted of counterfeiting in England and sent to the New World's plantations for life. Dean was purchased as an indentured servant by Alexander Spotswood of Germanna, Virginia, but he escaped in 1737 and was set loose upon an unsuspecting America. How many coins he counterfeited in the next few years has never been determined.

In the winter of 1770 Captain Blickenden of the ship *Trotman* brought his vessel into port at Annapolis, Maryland, carrying a band of counterfeiters who had been convicted in England and sent to the colonies as punishment. The coiners had been busy on the voyage across the Atlantic, making counterfeit dollars and shillings. Within a few hours after the *Trotman* came to port, the *Maryland Gazette* announced that counterfeit dollars and shillings were being passed around Annapolis at an alarming rate.

From the beginning of trade between the mother country and the North American colonies, counterfeiting flourished in America. One reason was that trade was carried on by means of private bills of credit, drawing on individuals for payment for merchandise delivered. A bill of credit might be worth several thousand pounds, and it could be cashed by nearly anyone, if the name of the merchant was familiar in the countinghouse. The counterfeiting had to be done by someone familiar with the inside workings of the countinghouse, and someone who had access to real bills of credit.

This counterfeiting was carried out quite successfully because bills of credit were not usually very carefully made. For a long time, bankers were careless in their scrutiny of the paper. Also, the voyage between England and an American port took several weeks, and so there was no quick way of apprehending the criminals. By the time the crime was discovered the criminals were usually long gone to some other part of the country.

One of the famous counterfeiters of bills of trade was Peter Long of Philadelphia. In 1739 he sent directions to England for the counterfeiting of the trade bills of the colonial government of New Jersey. The plates were made in England (where there was no punishment for such an action), and the bills were brought back to North America. Soon a brisk trade had developed.

In the summer of 1704 there occurred in Boston one of the most celebrated of early counterfeiting trials. It involved Peregrine White, Jr., son of the Peregrine White who was the *Mayflower* baby and firstborn New Englander. One day young Peregrine White and his son, Benoni, were arrested for passing counterfeit coins. They had succumbed to the blandishments of a professional counterfeiter named Thomas Odell, a slender, middle-sized man with black hair, who had the odd habit of holding his head on one side as he walked. When Peregrine White described his tempter, the officers knew just the man they should look for.

Odell escaped, but the shamefaced Peregrine White, who had been known as an honest Boston blacksmith, not only turned government evidence and confessed all, but he set off personally on the manhunt.

Peregrine White helped capture Odell in Stonington, Connecticut, where Odell was put in jail. He escaped and fled to Philadelphia. He was captured again and sent to Boston aboard the sloop *Derick Adolph*. When the ship touched at Newport, Odell managed to loosen his fetters and escaped once more. He was again captured after hiding for a week in a barn, and finally the authorities delivered him to Boston to be tried. He was convicted of counterfeiting, and sent to jail for a year and fined £300. A reward of £50 was given for this conviction. Who got it? Peregrine White, Jr., got it. But since he was accused of passing false coins, he was fined £30. So he profited by only £20 for turning in his companion.

Among the many gangs of counterfeiters who flourished in America in the eighteenth century was the Derby Gang, which operated in Derby, Connecticut. Samuel Weed, the brother of a respected physician, was the leader of this gang. Yet the doctor was not as respectable as he seemed, for he served as the "front man" for the gang. Dr. Weed's job was to secure agents to pass the money. Brother Samuel's forte was his ability to forge any man's signature and to make bills that looked like the real thing. But Dr.

... And More Counterfeit

Weed, Samuel, and many of their accomplices were arrested and sent to jail in the end.

Another counterfeiter of note was Joseph Bill, for a time a fellow prisoner of the Derby Gang in Hartford jail. Bill had been counterfeiting the Connecticut four-shilling bill. One day in Connecticut, Bill was arrested. When he was searched, some unfinished counterfeit money was found on his person. He admitted that he had made a plate from some pieces of copper and a crucible and had used an engraving tool to make the likeness of the money, "just for amusement" while he was spending some time all alone in the Connecticut woods near Cheshire. He had never signed or passed the bills, he said. (In those days bills were actually signed in ink by someone in authority.)

While the authorities were pondering his alibi, Bill met a young man named Abel Clark in jail, who was also awaiting trial. Clark was a member of the Derby Gang. One night the two of them escaped and made their way to Boston, where they quickly found another group of counterfeiters, led by Isaac Jones. Clark knew just where to look, because Jones was a counterfeiter of some note. He had made a number of copies of the seven-shilling Connecticut note and passed them successfully for months. Clark and Bill joined forces with Isaac Jones. Thus was born the infamous Massachusetts Gang. (Clark later dropped out of the gang and out of sight.)

The gang first set out to find a number of men to pass the money. That was one of the most difficult and dangerous parts of counterfeiting, where the gang leaders always took care. A perfect passer was one who never lost his aplomb, and if he was arrested, he never talked. But there were very few perfect passers. The closest Jones and Bill came to one was in the person of Jonathan Bryant, a shingle maker in Boston with a gift of gab. After a few meetings, they asked Bryant to join them, and he became head of the gang's passers.

The Massachusetts Gang then set up in business. Joseph Bill and Isaac Jones established the manufacturing works on an almost deserted spot, Long Island, near Boston. They made Massachusetts three-pound bills, Massachusetts ten-shilling bills, and Connecticut seven-shilling bills. Jonathan Bryant set about recruiting passers while his partners created the money. He recruited passers in Boston and Cambridge. Then he went to Hartford and New Haven in Connecticut. The Connecticut men seemed all right, but apparently Jonathan Bryant had been careless in his reading of their "characters." Two of them, David Wilcox, Jr., and Elias Wilcox, were caught. Instead of honoring the code, they implicated Bryant.

The Connecticut officers sent an agent to Massachusetts. He told the Massachusetts Bay Colony authorities the story of the counterfeiters as they had it from the captured men. One night the sheriff's men raided Jonathan Bryant's house and found ninety-five three-pound bills, nine seven-shilling bills, and thirty-two ten-shilling Massachusetts notes. Everyone of them was counterfeit, but so well made that the authorities might have been taken in had they not known the truth.

Jonathan Bryant appeared cheerful and helpful. He said he would take the officers to discover the hiding place of Joseph Bill and Isaac Jones. But Jonathan Bryant was true to the thieves' code. Somehow he managed to get word to the other counterfeiters. Bill and Jones fled before the officials arrived.

The officers picked up the trail of the two counterfeiters, however, and followed them to Newton Woods, Massachusetts. There they had taken up their business again and were busy making new "money." They were captured with their plates and taken to Cambridge jail.

Jails must have been very weak in those days, because almost immediately the two prisoners escaped. They met a friendly Indian, bribed him, and he guided them to the house of Jedediah Ashcraft in Groton, Connecticut. Bill identified himself as Dr. Wilson, a famous physician of the day. Jones said he was Captain Wright, another famous man, a hero who had lost his ship in the war against the French. The two said they must get to Sag Harbor, Long Island, very quickly. They spun a tale of bravery and derring-do and convinced Ashcraft, who took them across Long Island Sound in his own boat. There the counterfeiters made merry at Zeb Howel's tavern, passing bad notes and drinking good wine. Then, before the counterfeit was discovered, they dropped out of sight.

Some New York officials thought they had crossed the trail of the two one day when a Narragansett man was arrested in New York City for passing twenty-shilling bills of New York. He identified the maker of the bills as a Dr. Dustin, and the description sounded very much like Joseph Bill. But there was a real Dr. Dustin, who was also a counterfeiter. The Narragansett man hanged himself in his cell with his garters (rather than be hanged by New York authorities). Finally Joseph Bill was captured, but Isaac Jones escaped. Bill got off because he could blame everything on Dr. Dustin, who was captured by the New York sheriff and then escaped. Dr. Dustin disappeared along with Isaac Jones. Bill remained at large for another twenty years before he was again captured for counterfeiting at Albany and was finally hanged.

One of the most famous and most dangerous counterfeiters of colonial America was Owen Sullivan, head of the infamous Dover Money Club, which made counterfeit money in Dover, New York. Sullivan had for a time been a Boston goldsmith. Unfortunately he had tastes far beyond the means of a normal goldsmith. Yet he always seemed to have plenty of money. Of course the people around him wondered where his money came from, and one night, a bit the worse for drink, his wife was heard to remark scathingly that her husband was "a forty-thousand-pound money maker." This odd remark interested many who overheard it, including an officer of the law. Soon the officer found an excuse to pick Sullivan up. In jail they discovered a number of false ten-shilling notes in Sullivan's pocket. They came to the conclusion that he was competing illegally with the colonial finance officers. They were certain of the fact when a search of Sullivan's house unearthed a mold for casting coins, a vat of ink, and many reams of paper plus some partly printed sheets on which were forged the names of the signers of Massachusetts bills.

Sullivan was sent to jail in Boston. He did not have much to do, so he occupied his time in cutting a plate for counterfeit 40-shilling New Hampshire bills. He gave the plate to a man named Fairservice in return for promises to help him get out of jail. But Fairservice was caught, and the plates were captured. More evidence. The trial proceeded. In September, 1750, Sullivan was convicted, and sentenced to stand in the public pillory for two hours and to receive twenty lashes. This punishment was inflicted on him on September 13.

After his punishment, Sullivan moved to Providence, Rhode Island, organized a gang, and for two years successfully counterfeited the Rhode Island £16 bills. He and his gang were finally caught, and sentenced to have their ears cropped, to be branded on each cheek with an R, and to be sent to prison for various terms. The branding and the ear cropping were the important matters, for the branding would forever mark the man as a rogue, and the ear cropping would do so even more conspicuously. But then, there were brandings and brandings and ear croppings and ear croppings, and Sullivan, great rogue that he was, managed by bribery of the executioner to have his branding done so far back on his head that it was concealed by his hair, and his ears so slightly cropped that no one could be sure that he had not cut himself while shaving. While the others were being punished, he escaped. A confederate had smuggled him a cutlass. He beat his way through the crowd that had come to watch. The authorities chased and captured him. But a few days later Owen Sullivan escaped once more. This time he made his way into New York State to found the Dover Money Club.

At Dover the gang made counterfeit currency to imitate the paper money of nearly all the New England colonies. Owen Sullivan sent men into those colonies to pass the money and bring back the loot. In July, 1753, the Dover

119

Money Club moved to Killingley, Connecticut, and set up the counterfeiting shop there in the house of Jedediah Cady. That unlucky man was almost immediately caught trying to pass the counterfeit money, along with an Indian named Jeremiah Lisha.

Owen Sullivan seemed to bear a charmed life. He had gotten away on the day of surprise and chase. Soon he was back in Dover. He hired as agent a mason named John Clark, of Stratford, Connecticut, when the mason came to Dover to find work. The mason's trade was an excellent cover. Soon Clark was back in Stratford circulating bogus £8 Rhode Island notes. Others of the Money Club developed a ring of passers in other Connecticut towns, in Rhode Island, and covered nearly all of New York colony outside the city of New York. The club even established a subsidiary that counterfeited Spanish dollars, and for several years the club flooded New England with bogus money, both paper and coin. In the fall and winter of 1754 Sullivan printed £15,000 in bogus money from one set of plates alone, in a small shack in New Hampshire. That effort respresented only a fractional part of the counterfeiting ring's work. In the fall of 1755 four of Sullivan's passers were arrested in Newport, Rhode Island, with some £40,000 in bogus currency in hand.

At that time the gang may have had as much money in circulation as the legitimate governments it imitated.

But the tide was about to turn. The club victimized a law-abiding citizen of New Haven named Cornet Eliphalet Beacher. He did not take it lying down. He complained in person to the Connecticut legislature, and then set about agitating that the lawbreakers be brought to the bar of justice. He secured a warrant for the arrest of Sullivan and his friends. Then he personally began tracking down and seizing passers, and making citizen's arrests. He spent the next ninety-five days on horseback, organizing posses in three states, appearing before judges, capturing passers, always pursuing the elusive Sullivan and his gang, between Dutchess County, New York, and Connecticut.

One day early in 1755, Beacher overheard a pair of Dutchess County tavern keepers talking about Sullivan. Suspicious, he came back to the tavern several times, spent lavishly, and one day changed a large bill. When Beacher got out into the bright daylight, he saw that he had been given some counterfeit bills among his change. He returned to the tavern and accused the innkeepers of belonging to the band. He was so furious and so determined that he frightened them. They tried to persuade him to give the bad bills back and forget it all, but he pulled a gun and forced them to go off with him to the house of the local magistrate. There the innkeepers told all they knew about the Money Club. Most important, they revealed the location of the headquarters.

One of the suspects led them to the gang's headquarters. They went through a swamp and then thick woods, where the guide moved a pile of brush from the side of a hill, and they entered a large cave. Inside, in the back, Beacher found a long room, with wooden floor and plank walls, furnished with tables and chairs. A skylight had been cut through the hill to light the room.

They found the place, but not the bird. Sullivan had flown. He had learned that his accomplices had been arrested and had fully expected that they would betray the hiding place. He fled into the mountains and hid there for a week. Then, driven by hunger, he sought shelter in a farmhouse.

Beacher, meanwhile, was leading his band of vigilantes, searching every house in the region. In the middle of the night he came to the farmhouse. The family said they knew nothing of Sullivan. But Beacher saw some dirt that had recently been piled outside the house.

Beacher and his men then began to search. Beneath one bed they found loose planks. The plank was taken up, and Beacher found a passage beneath it. "Come out and surrender," he shouted.

He was right—it *was* Sullivan and he *did* come out. There was nothing else to do.

Owen Sullivan offered Beacher a fortune to let him escape. He had counterfeited hundreds of thousands of pounds, he said, and he could counterfeit any money ever made. Beacher would not listen. Sullivan then promised that he could make a counterfeit proof plate. He would do so for the authorities if they would let him go free. The answer was no. Sullivan was taken to New York City were he was tried for counterfeiting under harsh New York laws. He was convicted and sentenced to be hanged on the morning of May 7.

On the day of the hanging someone cut down the gallows, and they had to be rebuilt. So the fatal event was postponed, and postponed again. In the interim Sullivan made a speech, warning his confederates (there were twenty-nine of them, he said) to give up counterfeiting. He would not betray them by name, although he urged them, however, to destroy the plates and mend their ways.

When the gallows was rebuilt and the time came for him to pay his price, he mounted the scaffold with a large cud of tobacco in his mouth. He turned around to the watchers and smiled.

For all his thousands of pounds of counterfeit, the authorities found nothing of his fortunes except a saddle valued at £5. Eliphalet Beacher, the avenging angel of government, continued to try to round up the rest of the gang. He hunted down and supervised the prosecution of a few, but most of the gang either escaped, or forfeited bonds in one colony and ran away to another to live. The plates were never discovered. It was never really learned just how much damage the Dover Money Club had done to the currency of the New England colonies.

13
How the British Wrecked the Dollar

The temptation to wreak havoc among the enemy during time of war by ruining his currency is as old as war itself. It has not been practiced too often, not so much because it is impossible to counterfeit the moneys of other nations as because the game can be played by all concerned, and it can become a most dangerous game. By common consent the nations of the world have usually refrained from this warfare.

There have been exceptions. One of these was counterfeiting by the British government during the Revolutionary War. From the British point of view this might be excused by saying that His Majesty's government never accepted until near the end the fact that this was a revolution. Particularly in the beginning, the feeling officially was that all the trouble in the colonies was caused by a handful of malcontents, and if they could be hanged quickly enough, everything would return to normal.

How the British Wrecked the Dollar

After hostilities broke out in 1775, a pair of Tories came to the British and offered to counterfeit the currency of the insurgent Americans. They were Dr. Benjamin Church and his brother-in-law, a printer named John Fleming. So, in the first week of January, 1776, a printing press began turning out counterfeit copies of the $30 bill issued by Congress. The counterfeiters made their money aboard H.M.S. *Phoenix,* a forty-four gun ship lying in New York Harbor.

When the British captured New York City, it became the headquarters for British counterfeiting of American currency. General Howe quite approved this psychological and economic warfare. A New York newspaper on April 14, 1777, carried the following note:

> Persons going into other Colonies may be supplied with any number of counterfeit Congress-notes, for the Price of the Paper per Ream. They are so neatly and exactly executed that there is no Risque in getting them off, it being almost impossible to discover that they are not genuine. This has been proved by Bills to a very large Amount which have already been successfully circulated. Enquire for Q.E.D. at the Coffee-House, from 11 P.M. to 4 A.M. during the present months.

The Americans were indignant. An intelligence agent informed General George Washington that a new group of bills was about to be distributed, but very little could be done to stop it. It never was stopped. An American privateer captured a British ship which carried a letter from Sir Henry Clinton to Lord George Germain, British Secretary of State, in which the counterfeiting was openly discussed. In April, 1780, two British ships were captured off Sandy Hook—the *Blacksnake* and the *Morning Star*. When they were brought into Egg Harbor on the New Jersey coast, they were found to contain large sums of counterfeit Continental currency. A raid on a house near Sandy Hook lighthouse unearthed 45,000 counterfeit Continental dollars and eight counterfeiters.

The British circulated their counterfeit in many ways. One day in January, 1778, General Howe sent a wagonload of supplies for British soldiers who were being held prisoner of war by the Americans. The wagons left Philadelphia under a flag of truce. They were stopped by the Americans because two more British officers were in the train than were listed on the orders.

During the discussions it began to rain, and two of the bags of "provisions" were soaked. The Americans opened them to see what might be salvaged, and discovered that the bags were filled with bogus Continental money. When the wagon train was searched, four drivers were discovered to be carrying large sums of Continental counterfeit.

Some of the counterfeiters and the passers of counterfeit were well-known men of the colonies. One of the Tories was James Smither, a prominent Philadelphia printer and engraver before the war. When the British left Philadelphia, he left with them—luckily for him, because Congress had charged him with treason.

Loyalists or Tories were also the principal passers of counterfeit. One of these was Colonel Stephen Holland of Londonderry, New Hampshire, a red-faced, pockmarked man, about five feet eight inches tall, who had retired from the army in 1762 and had settled down to become a merchant and tavern keeper. In 1775 he owned ten thousand acres of New Hampshire land and was regarded as a wealthy man. He was a good friend of Governor John Wentworth. When the colonies rebelled, Wentworth persuaded Holland to remain in New Hampshire and work for the British cause, so Holland organized a counterfeiting ring, to bring confusion to his fellow countrymen. For many months various Tories who were not known to be in league with the enemy traveled around the colonies, occasionally striking some key point where they were given quantities of counterfeit money. One day one of this gang stopped in Wallingford, Connecticut, to buy some flax, and also to deliver some letters to a courier who would take them on to the British authorities. This man, John Moore, of Peterborough, was just coming down with smallpox. He collapsed, and after a few days' illness he died. Before he died he secreted his damning letters under a stone in the barn of the farm where he was staying. A few days later a small boy looking for eggs found the stone and the package of letters. They revealed Stephen Holland as a traitor and proved that he and others were in league with Governor Wentworth.

Two members of this gang were caught in Danbury, Connecticut, and taken to the headquarters of General Enoch Poor. There the American revolutionaries discovered that the two were carrying some ten thousand counterfeit Continental dollars. They confessed that they had passed fifty thousand more. These two, David Farsworth of Hollis and John Blair of Holderness, were tried, convicted, and executed for treason at Hartford.

Many other Tories were captured, but many escaped.

Holland was captured and escaped. He was recaptured, tried, and convicted and sentenced to death. He escaped again from prison in Exeter. He reached the British lines, where he was welcomed and given a commission in the intelligence service. John Longdon, a New Hampshire patriot, lamented his escape. "Damn him . . ." he said, "I hope to see him hanged. He has done more damage than ten thousand men could have done."

Benjamin Franklin said the counterfeiters were using the most effective possible method of destroying the value of the American money. He was troubled, because the British effort had been enormously successful. The British so debased the American currency with their millions of Continental forgeries that George Washington once wrote John Jay that "a wagon load of money will scarcely purchase a wagon load of provisions." So desperate did the situation grow that in the spring of 1781 an angry mob in Philadelphia paraded up the streets with paper money stuck in their hats and a dog tarred and plastered all over with the Continental currency. The phrase "not worth a Continental" became a part of the American vocabulary, and the British counterfeiters were very much responsible for that.

14
The Billion-Dollar Plan

The most extensive counterfeiting operation in the history of the world was carried out during World War II. The Germans were theoretically working against the Allies, but the effort deteriorated into a matter of personal gain of the conspirators.

The idea came to a Nazi official named Alfred Naujocks one day in 1940 as he sat in his office in the Reichssicherheits Hauptamt, the German Security Service. The British had just air-dropped thousands of German ration cards on several cities in the Third Reich in an effort to confuse the Reich's economy. The German Ministry of Economics had informed Naujocks but had not taken it very seriously because the fake ration cards were so badly counterfeited that any ration office could immediately spot them.

But Naujocks decided he should fight fire with fire. He

proposed that the German government forge a £ billion in British currency and then drop the notes over the British Isles, thus really wrecking the British economy. He envisaged an almost total collapse and a quick surrender. Naujocks soon found it would be quite possible to forge British notes on a large scale—difficult but possible. He went to his superior, Reinhard Heydrich, with the idea, Heydrich went to Hitler, and Hitler approved. So *Unternehmen Andreas,* or Operation Andrew, was launched.

Naujocks went then to the secret printing office, where the security service produced forged passports and other faked documents needed by spies overseas. The head of this laboratory was a man named Bernhard Kruger. Soon the planners decided that £5 notes were to be the staple production. The paper of real British notes was analyzed in half a dozen laboratories. The type faces were reproduced and specially cast in metal. Notes were enlarged twenty times, to be used as guides for the finest engravers in Germany.

They were not far along when it became apparent that the paper of the British notes was so difficult to make it would have to be fabricated by hand. But neither expense nor effort were to be spared in this project, and soon Naujocks had a special team working at a secret paper factory at Spechthausen, near Berlin. Eventually the workers produced a paper that even under the microscope was almost identical with the paper of the British notes. Only under ultraviolet light could the difference be seen —the British paper appeared bright lilac and the German paper was gray. The Germans discovered this failure, and it was back to the laboratory. After several months the technicians found that the "pure" flax supplied by German manufacturers was not pure and that the British flax was imported from Turkey. The Germans then bought Turkish flax and made a paper that was better, but still not good enough. Naujocks reasoned that the British paper makers were using old rags, while the Germans were using new flax. So the flax was made into rags, sent out to be dirtied, washed, and then brought back to be made into paper. This did the trick. When the German counterfeit was compared to the British original, no difference could be found in the laboratory.

In the summer of 1940 the engravers managed to perfect the plates. Even when their design was enlarged ten times and examined with magnifying glasses for discrepancies, none were found. The experts had created as perfect a forgery as could be made.

Heydrich then began to study the passing of the forged currency. He soon learned that the only safe way was to people who would normally be in position to handle large amounts of foreign money and thus would not come under suspicion in the various countries of Europe where the British pounds were to be passed.

In the spring of 1941 the Germans were ready for their last test. They sent an agent into Switzerland with a bundle of British £5-note forgeries. The agent carried a letter from the Deutsche Reichsbank, asking the help of the Swiss banking authorities in discovering whether or not these notes were forgeries. The Swiss examined the notes carefully for three days, and reported. *The notes were genuine,* they said. Pretending to be uncertain, the agent asked the Swiss to check with the Bank of England, to see if the notes had actually been issued by them. *The Bank of England certified the notes as genuine.* So the way was clear for the Germans to begin their counterfeiting on a vast scale.

Just as the technical operation was ready, the counterfeiting organization fell apart. Naujocks was found to be mixed up with another German official in illegal gold dealings for personal profit. Heydrich was furious. He fired Naujocks and disbanded his ring. The counterfeiters had produced £500,000 in forged British notes. They had worked against great odds for eighteen months, and in one move the operation seemed to be destroyed.

Heydrich chose the laboratory man Bernhard Kruger to rejuvenate the counterfeiting plan, and renamed it Operation Bernhard. Kruger was ordered to begin production somewhere near Berlin, and he chose the Sachsenhausen concentration camp. Overnight his organization vanished. His workers deserted—they would not enter a concentration camp, no matter what the reason.

Kruger had to start all over. He had the plates, paper, some printed notes, and a new complication. After the Germans conquered nearly all of western Europe, the Security Service people had unleashed forged £5 notes on the markets in Paris. The flood of new money had played hob with the French economy. The German Ministry of Economics complained and demanded that the process be stopped.

As the authorities considered this complication, a retired German businessman named Friedrich Schwend suggested that the forged pounds be used to finance German intelligence work throughout the world. By this time Walter Schellenberg had replaced Heydrich as head of the security service, and he agreed with Schwend.

The counterfeiting system would be incredibly complex, involved as it was with the German espionage system. It demanded the use of double agents, dishonest businessmen in neutral and Allied countries, and in countries dominated by the Reich, and even the use of the Chetniks of Yugoslavia, who sometimes got arms from the British and the Americans and sold them to the Germans for forged British pounds.

Some of the forged money stuck to the pockets of agents. Their forged pounds bought Swiss francs, then they converted these into diamonds or to numbered accounts in Swiss banks.

By 1943 the counterfeiting operation was in full swing, reaching down into Italy. The idea of dropping millions of pounds on Britain had disappeared from everyone's mind. It was too complicated. If the Germans did this to the British, the British would leave no stone unturned to reciprocate, and the German currency was far easier to duplicate successfully than the British pound. But by using counterfeit British pounds to finance an expensive overseas espionage system, Schwend estimated that the secret service could have an independent income of 250 million Reichsmarks a year, and in the end the British would pay the bill. The thought pleased the Germans.

At Sachsenhausen the order came: more production. Forty prisoners who had experience as engravers or printers were promised good treatment if they would work to produce the notes. This operation was so secret that these men were confined to a special area of the camp.

As for the passing organization, Schwend undertook that task on a strictly business basis. He guaranteed that he would finance the sales organization and operate at his own risk, for a share of the profits. He employed a chief agent who took 25 percent and split that with the passers. Schwend took 8.33 percent—and estimated that this would bring him £83,000 a month personally.

Soon the demand for counterfeit pounds was greater than the supply. Schellenberger asked for the production of £50 notes. Kruger objected. If they produced such large notes, he said, something was bound to go wrong. They could not control the serial numbers of the legitimate notes. Bankers were much more likely to check serial numbers on large notes. What if someone found that he had two notes with exactly the same serial number? Obviously then someone would smell a rat. The word would soon be out through the underworld—and the whole counterfeiting program might collapse.

Still the demand was so great that Schellenberger insisted that the £50 notes be produced; so they were.

Three qualities of notes were used. Only those of the first quality (and they were examined a dozen times) would be used by German agents in enemy countries and German businessmen in neutral countries. These notes defied detection by anyone except a British treasury agent. Second-quality notes were used for collaborators in occupied countries (which shows what the Germans thought of *them*) and for black-market operations. Third-quality notes were kept for small deals with unimportant people.

When Mussolini was rescued by Colonel Skorzeny, the

way was paved through the use of fifty thousand forged British pounds, paid out for information as to Mussolini's whereabouts. The Germans bought British and American arms from the Chetniks of Yugoslavia, once paying £100,000 for arms that included heavy weapons. Schwend negotiated one deal that ran to £2.5 million sterling. In Turkey, the butler of the British ambassador was seduced with counterfeit British pounds (£300,000) into spying on his employer. The information was good, if the money was not. That operation, called Operation Cicero, resulted in the Germans' being warned of air raids on the oil fields of Ploesti, even down to dates. The Ploesti raids turned out to be one of the most disastrous American air efforts of the war, partly because of counterfeit money.

Not all the money was so well spent. In Trieste, two men and one woman—agents of the counterfeit ring— tried to make off with £2.5 million of the bogus money in the spring of 1944, when it was apparent that the Germans were losing the war. They failed and were executed on the spot. After the second front opened in June, 1944, the Nazi bigwigs used the false pounds to buy jewelry, paintings, anything that they could put aside for the coming "rainy days." Rembrandt's "Man With a Sword" was purchased by one Nazi with bogus pounds. The joke was on the buyer, this time. This painting was also a forgery, by the Dutchman Han van Meegeren. He forged many great works during the war years and passed them off on such notables as Hermann Goering.

The pounds were sometimes sold in lots of £250,000 by dealers in Switzerland to international bankers and businessmen. No one could possibly know how many wealthy Europeans were swindled, because most of the activity involved was shady if not actually illegal, and the swindled had no real recourse against the German government.

As the war drew to an end, Schwend, who was the brains of the sales organization, made plans to get out of Germany. He brought hundreds of thousands of forged English pounds into Switzerland, and with them bought houses and apartment houses and other properties all over Europe, and even in South America. He bought French twenty-franc gold pieces. He bought jewels, including pieces made for the last Czar of Russia.

When the United States entered the war, the Germans also began to produce excellent forgeries of American $100 bills. The initial target was for production of ten thousand such bills, or $1 million. Already many millions of British pounds had been produced and passed. In December, 1944, when the war was going badly, the counterfeiting apparatus was removed from Sachsenhausen to the Mauthausen camp near Linz, Austria. In May, 1945, matters were so desperate that it was decided to put an end to Operation Bernhard. The equipment was bundled up and packed into three trucks and trailers. One truck broke down near Redl-Zipf on the River Traun, and its contents were pushed into the river. The contents of the other trucks were dumped into the Toplitzsee, and not until much later were some of the British notes recovered by skin divers from the icy waters of the lake. Schwend, the chief passer, made his own deal with the British and American military leaders, and finally reached South America, where he had been very careful to make heavy investments with his share of the millions of dollars' worth of bogus pounds he had supervised. He took up residence quietly as a wealthy citizen of Lima, Peru.

How many Bernhard pounds were issued remained a secret, then and forever. In 1959 and afterward, the British and the Americans made some discoveries, but they never learned the total extent of the production. The notes continued to circulate until the British government changed the design of its currency. Even in the 1960's it was still thought that these Bernhard pounds were used in clandestine work behind the Iron Curtain. It was the greatest swindle ever perpetrated by counterfeiters—by one government against its enemies, its friends, and its servants.

15
The New Collectors

Many numismatists have said that coin collecting has become a madness in the last half of the twentieth century. The old-line numismatists are not very happy, either, about some trends that have become apparent in the 1960's and 1970's.

What displeased the old timers was what is sometimes called "sharpshooting"—accumulating or hoarding. This practice is one of the most common marks of coin collecting in the twentieth century, and the direction is indicated by advertisements in a number of numismatic publications.

One such advertisement pointed out that a wise person should invest $2,500 in coins for each year for the next ten years. This particular dealer would invest these in new coins for the investor. Then, at the expiration of ten years the investor would sell the first year's coins, and the next year sell the next year's coins, etc., etc., while continuing to buy new lots of coins each year. Each ten years, based on previous records, the coins would appreciate five times in value, or 500 percent. And so, said the advertisement, the lucky investor could retire at the end of ten years of such investment with an income of $10,000 each year for life, simply by investing his original $2,500 each year.

This plan, of course, suggests that the coins would increase in value five times in ten years—and the advertiser could make quite a good case for this plan on the basis of the record of rolls of coins and their values. A roll of San Francisco 1949 dimes went from $8 in 1953 to $300 in 1963. There were more spectacular rises—of a roll of 1931 San Francisco cents rising in value from $90 to $4,000, of a bag of 1960 pennies (small dates) rising from $2,000 to $20,000.

But the fact was that many of these huge increases in values were caused by the huge increase in the number of coin collectors in the period. Could and would the collection of coins increase steadily from that time on? It could and might continue for a time, until some disaster wiped out some of these speculators. Then the mania would lose it attractiveness to the sharpshooters, and the numismatists, who had been sitting by, watching some wild speculation, would settle down to feel a bit more comfortable.

Many who call themselves coin collectors sneer at those who buy American coins in rolls and save them. The major reason for collecting in this fashion is simply to make profits, and though there is nothing wrong with that, collectors do not like to think of the debasement of their hobby.

Coins, Collectors and Counterfeiters

Like stamp collecting, sometimes the roll buyers may be fooled—but not often, because coins in past years have had a considerable intrinsic value, unlike stamps, which are nothing but pieces of paper. Coin collectors have not had the same bad luck that stamp collectors had, for example, with the National Parks issues of the 1930's. Many bought hundreds of sheets of these stamps, so many that the stamps did not increase in value anything like the manner in which they had been expected to increase.

In the 1970's coin collecting faced some of these dangers—the major danger being that some economic dislocation might throw hundreds of thousands of hoarded rolls of coins onto the market, and thus decrease their value. It was not unusual for a hoard of coins to wreak real havoc, as with those silver dollars that the federal government put on the market, ruining the investments of some collectors.

The huge increases are always featured by some advertisers, particularly the roll dealers. They could show how in a year coin rolls increased two, three, four, five, or more times in value. It was hard to find coin rolls that did not increase somewhat in value, because they had an intrinsic value as metal, and they had a value as coins as well. Some of these dealers advertised that collectors could earn as much as 100 percent per year by investing in rolls, and undoubtedly it was done.

Coin collecting in the 1970's had become a big business. In 1960 Michael DiSalle, the former governor of Ohio, made news by going into the coin business in a big way, as chairman of the board of the Paramount International Coin Corporation of Ohio. This company started out with a bang by making a million-dollar stock offer to the public. It was not a trick corporation at all—it would be engaged in the business of buying, managing, and selling unusual and rare coins. It was the very first coin company to "go public," that is, to become so large a business that it would register with the Securities and Exchange Commission and sell stock, in the open market. It was a very good indication of what had happened to a minor hobby in less than twenty years.

If there were any statistics to show the holdings of coin collectors, they would be argued over for years by the collectors themselves, but one thing seemed plain: Coin collectors, by and large, tended to have a greater investment in their collections and to be more concerned with money values than stamp collectors and some other collectors. (Collectors of rare paintings and speculators in art were certainly more inclined to be sharpshooters.) And yet . . .

Consider the case of Mrs. L. Botha of Tweefontein colliery, Witbank, South Africa. Mrs. Botha was not a coin collector, but there were lots of people in the Union of South Africa who were coin collectors, and she made a small fortune by selling off some tickeys—three-penny bits used in the Union to make telephone calls.

Mrs. Botha had a habit of saving tickeys for rainy days. One day some friend who was a coin collector told her to be on the lookout for a 1931 tickey, because only 128 of them had been minted. The friend apparently did not tell her that of the 128 tickeys, 125 had already been accounted for, leaving three tickeys on the loose. But one day Mrs. Botha looked at a tickey in her hand, and sure enough, it was a 1931 tickey. She went to the collector's literature and discovered that her coin was worth 480 rands, or about $720 in American money. She advertised it for R480 in the newspapers and soon had many takers. Then she was not so sure she wanted to sell, because after all, she had one of the rare coins, of which only two others were still on the loose.

That is how collectors are made.

Bibliography

Brown, Laurence, *Coins Through the Ages*. New York: Sterling Publishing Co., 1962.

Brown, M. R., and Dunn, J. W., *A Guide to the Grading of United States Coins*. Racine, Wis.: n.p., 1964.

Burgess, F. W., *Chats on Old Coins*. London: T. Fisher Unwin, 1919.

Coffin, Joseph, *Coin Collecting*. New York: Coward McCann, 1938.

————*The Complete Book of Coin Collecting*. New York: Coward McCann, 1959.

Coin Collecting for Fun and Profit. New York: Coin World, 1964.

Crump, Irving, *Our United States Secret Service*. New York: Dodd, Mead, 1948.

Bibliography

Del Mar, Alex, *A History of the Precious Metals*. New York: Cambridge Encyclopedia Company, 1902.

French, Charles F., *U. S. Coins*. New York: Cornerstone Library, 1975.

LaGrange, Francis, with William Murray, *Flag on Devil's Island*. Garden City, N.Y.: Doubleday and Company, 1961.

Mathews, G. D., *The Coinages of the World*. New York: Scott and Company, 1876.

Pirie, Anthony, *Operation Bernhard*. New York: William Morrow & Co., 1962.

Rawlins, Gertrude, *Coins and How to Know Them*. New York: Frederick A. Stokes, n.d.

Reinfeld, Fred, *Coin Collector's Handbook*. New York: Sterling Publishing Co., 1961.

————*A Treasury of American Coins*. Garden City, N.Y.: Hanover House, 1961.

————*A Treasury of the World's Coins*. New York: Sterling Publishing Co., 1953.

————and Hobson, Burton, *Catalogue of the World's Most Popular Coins*. New York: Sterling Publishing Co., 1965.

Scott, Kenneth, *Counterfeiting in Colonial America*. New York: Oxford University Press, 1957.

Wang Yu-chuan, *Early Chinese Coinage*. New York: The American Numismatic Society, 1951.

Index

Coins, Collectors and Counterfeiters

Index

Index

Index

Index

Vermont, money of, 56
Viking coins in Britain, 24
Virginia tobacco notes, 54
Virtuoso's Companion, The, 63
Vollständiges Thaler Cabinet, 65

W
Wampum
    counterfeiting of, 49
    money use of, 49
Wartime
    British coinage during, 27
    counterfeiting in, 124
    German counterfeiting during, 129
    forgery of American currency, German, 136
White, Peregrine, Jr., counterfeiting scandal and, 113
Women and collecting, 64
World coin values, 85
World War II, German counterfeiting during, 129
World's Columbia Exposition, commemoratives of, 87

Y
Yen, Japanese, 44

Z
Zerbe, Farran, as collector, 91